One on the Seesaw

Random House New York

ONE ON THE SEESAW

The Ups and Downs of a Single-Parent Family

Carol Lynn Pearson

Grateful acknowledgment is made to Harper & Row, Publishers, Inc., for permission to reprint an excerpt from the poem "Little Abigail and the Beautiful Pony" from A *Light in the Attic* by Shel Silverstein. Copyright © 1981 by Evil Eye Music, Inc. Reprinted by permission of Harper & Row, Publishers, Inc.

Library of Congress Cataloging-in-Publication Data
Pearson, Carol Lynn.
One on the seesaw.
1. Single parents—United States. 2. Single-parent family—United States. 3. Fatherless family—United States. I. Title.
HQ759.915.P43   1988   306.8'56   88-42662
ISBN 0-394-56496-0

Manufactured in the United States of America
Typography and binding design by J. K. Lambert

9 8 7 6 5 4 3 2
First Edition

For
　　DONALD
　　DAVID
　　WARREN
　　AND MARIE
with whom I have
learned a lot
about family

Contents

Introduction

When I was insisting that Aaron eat something he didn't want to eat, John observed, "She's fattening you up, Aaron, just like she did to Hansel and Gretel."

Sure, you can laugh. They're not your kids calling you a witch after you've worked your fingers to the bone for them. We're all voyeurs, I guess, when it comes to other people's families. We like to peek in the window and laugh or sigh and then go on home to our own. That's why I wrote this book—so you could take a look at two families, mine and yours.

Mine is not a *Little House on the Prairie* family with pioneer charm and nostalgia, not an *Eight Is Enough* family with a glamorous social life and a startling number of children, not a

Bill Cosby family with a wise patriarch or an Erma Bombeck family with a witty matriarch.

My family is different. But most families these days are different, and so that makes us about average, I guess. When I was little, people used to talk about "broken homes" with the same tone of voice they used when talking about cancer, and I knew that "broken homes" were responsible for just about everything that was going wrong in the world.

My children live in such a home. But I don't think of it as broken, and I don't think they do either. The family stretched and cracked and, like the glass I watched take shape in Venice, had to be sent back to the fire and reblown. It's in a different shape now than the one I originally planned. But it's in good shape and it works.

Families these days come in all shapes. The "traditional" shape is the odd one now. Very much in the minority these days is the family in which the dad works and the mom stays home with the kids. More and more families are headed by single parents or have some other nontraditional variation on the family theme.

I certainly didn't get married with the anticipation of being a single parent. Nobody does, I suppose. My family, in fact, was going to be not only permanent but eternal. I met Gerald in 1965 in a play at Brigham Young University in Provo, Utah, and we were married the following year in the Mormon temple in Salt Lake City. Gerald was a wonderful, sensitive, energetic, charming, capable man. He was also a homosexual man. Our life together made a strange story, involving our mutual hope that marriage was the answer, our despair that it did not change his emotional makeup, having four children together, finally divorcing, though remaining good friends, and ultimately his death from AIDS in my home where I had been caring for him. *

* This story is told in *Good-bye, I Love You*, published by Random House in 1986.

For ten years now I have been a single parent. It hasn't been easy. But as I watch other families around me—the step-families, the blended families, and even the "traditional" families with their particular challenges (and few there are that escape something pretty tough)—I know that no one has a corner on family problems, and there's no point in feeling sorry for ourselves. No one has a corner on happiness, either, or on being proud or silly. We're all of us, whatever shape our family takes, worth respecting, supporting, celebrating. And celebrating family is what this book is about.

—————

My family consists of one mother and four children. All of the children are blond and blue-eyed and nice-looking and—uninhibited. I have spent a lot of hours trying to cultivate some inhibitions in them, but to no avail.

Emily came first. She has just turned twenty and is a talented singer-dancer-actress, spending this year traveling with a performing group called "The Young Ambassadors" from Brigham Young University. Her room, in our house in the Bay Area of California, still smells of Paris perfume, even though she's home only occasionally. Emily is so sensitive that she cried at five to see a mouse in a trap and fainted at seventeen to see films of injuries in driver's training . . . so dramatic and volatile at fifteen that if I asked her if her homework was done she exploded and ran in tears to her room, making me wonder if we could possibly live together for three more years . . . so loving that she taught me how to say the words . . . so beautiful that a man in New York said to me, "Lady, I cannot watch you sign your traveler's check, I cannot take my eyes off your lovely daughter". . . so unselfconscious that she makes her "ugly" face upon request. Emily wants to be in love, to be a mother, and to win an Academy Award.

John is eighteen and has just graduated from high school. He is an artist, gentle, tender, helpful, and is planning to be a film animator and charms everyone with his great characters. He is also congenitally absent-minded and maddeningly argumentative when defending a point he thinks is important. He wears his hair long, his one mild rebellion, and he is even flirting with the idea of piercing one ear. (Though of course he would take the earring out when he went to church.) He is very good-looking and even shows some muscle on his slim arms when he wears the Rush T-shirt he cut the arms out of. John walks like he is still not used to being six-foot-three, lurching just a little like an animated figure that needs a few more frames per second. John's room smells slightly musty, like most boys' rooms smell, even when the dirty socks are raked away.

Aaron is seventeen and a senior at Las Lomas High. His bedroom is filled with guitars and his stereo and the speakers he has built himself and the weight-lifting equipment that has turned him into a real muscle man. Aaron snores. He looks the most like me of any of the children, which is the only reason I know for sure that he was not a changling: most of his traits and interests are strange to me. *I* would not play that kind of music and play it so loud. *I* would not grunt instead of speaking articulately. *I* would not rather spend a day with a hammer and saw than a book. But I love to watch Aaron's quick confidence and I envy his ability to deal with the material world. What would I do without him to fix the gate and change the oil and put the caulking around the bathtub? Aaron still loves to play little-boy tricks. A few days ago he shot my white sweater with red disappearing ink and grinned while I gasped. Shorter than John, Aaron is still taller than me and likes to pick me up and throw me on the couch, just like I did him when he was two. If you can bring yourself to appreciate Aaron's sense of humor, he is a great person to have around.

The fourth child, Katy, is thirteen and in the eighth grade at

Walnut Creek Intermediate. She always giggles when I lift her ponytail and kiss the back of her neck and say, "Oh, Katy, I'm *so* glad you are not a horse, or I could not *do* this!" Katy doesn't really want to *be* a horse, she just wants to live with them, to smell like them, to ride them. She is, in fact, earth mother to all creatures great and small, wants to be a veterinarian, and just now is specializing in a puppy and hamsters, which make her bedroom smell as good as it can smell without a horse in it. (I gave her a bottle of cologne for her birthday and later found it in the Goodwill box. "Oh, Katy, keep this," I said. "You'll want it in a few years." "Why?" she asked. "Will it smell better in a few years?") Katy is wildly disorganized and every piece of clothing she owns piles up dirty before she sends her laundry through. And Katy is a poet. After repenting of telling a lie, she said, "Mom, I think honesty is like soap. It covers you all over and makes you all clean." "Katy," I said, "you have a wonderful way of putting things. You could be a writer when you grow up." "Yes," she said, "sometimes I have this . . . this squirt of similies." That's what she'll be, a poetic veterinarian.

Those are my children. You'll learn more about them in the following chapters, and you may learn something about their mother too, and about family living in the eighties.

One on the Seesaw

1. Killing John's Birds

"John, you're crazy," I laughed after he had told me yet another of the wild schemes he'd thought up, a mousetrap made out of a sponge and water and grated cheese, fixed so that the mouse gets his teeth caught.

"Oh, no, Mom," John said with a serious smile. "I'm not crazy. I am imaginative and hopeful and spellbound!"

The upside of imaginative, hopeful, and spellbound is years of enjoying the marvelous creature that is John; the downside of those three adjectives is wondering if John would ever make it to fourth grade.

First the upside. Reverence is what I have felt when gazing at Michelangelo's "David," when listening to the great organ in the

Salt Lake Tabernacle, or when looking at my son John. His father and I used to delight in trading "Johnny stories," and imagining all the wonderful things he was going to do. Gerald always smiled as he remembered the evening four-year-old "Johnnycake" in his pajamas shot into the living room from the unlighted hall, shouting, "Here comes the little boy out of darkness!"

There has always been something bright about John, something clear and guileless that wins your heart immediately. Even a teacher who was climbing the blackboard over John said in a conference, "I love John. I would have to say about most students that I like them, but not about John. I *love* John. I see something quite wonderful in him."

At three John held his first wishbone. He listened to me tell him to make a wish, stared for a moment at the wishbone, and then took a deep breath . . . and blew.

At four he led us in a song at family time, saying, "We will now sing 'I Am a Child of God' because St. Patrick's Day is coming up."

At five John said, while playing with his milk, "If clouds were cows I would take my cup outside and fill it up and drink it down." And "Mom, you'd better get into the kitchen fast! The water on the stove is getting mad!"

At six he prayed at bedtime, "And bless me that I will learn to swim so that when a leopard or some other animal in the cat family is chasing me, I will say 'Thank you, Heavenly Father, for this animal in the cat family,' and then I will get in the water because leopards can't swim, and I will get away, so bless me that I will learn to swim."

At ten John called the police on his brother because Aaron and Scott were destroying the environment up at the creek by jumping off the tops of six-foot water pipes onto a board they had placed over the reeds to cushion their fall. I was with old friends visiting in the front room when John came in to announce,

"Mom, it is my duty to inform you that a policeman will be arriving here in about two minutes." I might have broken John's neck, except that a police officer was on his way. My friends thought it was funny. So did the police officer, who had a good visit with all the boys, explaining how one cares for the environment and when one calls in the law.

At twelve John wrote his will in the middle of the night because the pain from the occasional attacks of neuritis in his feet was so bad. "To my friend Davy Tate I leave thirty dollars, which is all I have, and my records and my chest of drawers if he wants it. And my posters to his brother Chris. For verification of this will, take it to Mrs. Sturgeon. She is my teacher and she knows my handwriting."

The upside of imaginative, hopeful, and spellbound goes on and on. John is a charming, generous, interesting person, who scrapes together fifty dollars to send me and a friend to see Liza Minnelli because he knows I love her, who tells his sisters how pretty they look, who even defends his brother when he's rude to him, and who quizzes me on his character, saying, "Mom, what things in me are you unhappy about, so I can try to correct them?"

———

The downside, however. The *downside*. That has to do with the spellbound part, I guess. John has always been caught in a spell, hypnotized by the dramas going on in his mind, unaware of what's happening around him, not always listening, forgetful, spaced out, losing so many lunch pails in elementary school that I considered just taping a sandwich to his shirt. John is very much like his mother, only his mother managed, early on, some heroic adaptation so that nobody ever had to wonder if she would make it to fourth grade.

The idea that any of my children would have trouble with school never, ever occurred to me. Bad grades happened in other families, like drug addiction and unwed pregnancies happened in other families. Surely my children would all bring home the straight A's that are in their genes.

When in John's second grade a number of "not satisfactory's" began to be checked on his report cards, along with comments like "John does not listen," or "Does not return homework," I was amazed. How could a child who was as clever and bright as John not do well in school?

It must be his teacher's fault, I figured. But at back-to-school night I had been very impressed with Mrs. Folin, an energetic, happy brunette who seemed to be very well organized. I made an appointment to visit with her and get this straightened out.

"John sits right here," she said, indicating a desk in the front row. "I moved him up here after the first week. You can sit there if it isn't too small for you."

"No, it's fine." I slid into the little desk, wanting to get John's perspective on everything, on his teacher, on the blackboard, on the rows of paper jack-o'-lanterns decorating the wall to my left. Each had the name of a pupil on it, and I skimmed the row looking for John's.

"John's isn't there," Mrs. Folin said apologetically. "He didn't get it finished in time."

"Oh."

"I'm so glad you came in, Mrs. Pearson," Mrs. Folin said with a little laugh, shaking her head. "John has got me puzzled. I love him! I just adore him! He's one of the most charming, delightful children I've ever seen. But he seems to be . . . somewhere else half the time. I ask him to take his turn at reading aloud—he's a very good reader—but he hasn't been following, so he doesn't know the place. I call for homework, and his is not handed in. I give an instruction and in a few minutes his hand goes up and he asks me what he's supposed to do. He's a dreamer, which is wonderful. But he doesn't pay attention and get things done, and that is not wonderful."

I felt myself getting smaller and smaller until I almost fit the desk. She was describing John, all right. And suddenly now, to hear it from a stranger, I felt all the alarms go off. I had become used to John's daydreaming, used to having to tell him two or three times to do something, used to hearing him say, "I forgot," used to him losing things. I had accepted all that as part of John's personality. Did I think things would be different at school? I had never been forced to grade him, never had to write out a report card for him, never had to articulate in a Comments section his flaws. But if I had had to, I would have seen and said exactly what Mrs. Folin had. I sighed and looked up at her. "You're right. What do we do?"

"Well, we just don't let him get away with it. We break him of some habits right now. We don't *let* him be irresponsible. I think we ought to have daily communication for a while. John will write down what the homework is, bring it to me and I'll initial the paper. Then he'll bring it home and show you, do the homework, and bring it back."

Simple enough. Certainly. How could there possibly be so many loopholes in a system that simple? How could John so often forget to have his teacher initial the homework paper? How could the paper magically diasppear from his pants pocket on the way home from school? How could he reply "I don't know" to the question "What happened to the homework?" so often and so sincerely?

He was not unwilling. He was never belligerent. He just sometimes . . . was not there. But he tried.

"How was school?" I would ask enthusiastically every day.

"Terrific."

"How about math?"

"Terrific."

"Did you get them all right?"

"Yes."

"Quick, what's eleven take away seven?"

Pause. "That's the only one I need to work on."

———

John made it to third grade, and to fourth, fifth, and sixth. And his teachers loved him and told me of the wonderful, creative contributions he made to the class. But . . . *but* he seemed to be somewhere else much of the time, and he didn't always get his work done. Each teacher brought me that information apologetically and as if maybe he or she was the first to notice it. My conferences at school felt like déjà vu.

One day John trudged in from fifth grade and said sorrowfully after I had given him a hug, "Mom, Mr. Davis calls me Spaceman. He gives everybody a nickname and that's mine. Spaceman. And now all the kids call me Spaceman." He looked at me as he would look at someone who had been scratched by a cat he had been playing with. He knew he deserved the title, unkind though it was, and he didn't expect me to defend him.

I wanted to, though. I wanted to take in my arms this boy, who was now nearly as tall as I, and squeeze him until he was little again and hold him safe against everything beyond the front steps, safe against a teacher who names him Spaceman and kids who tease, safe against his own stumbling. But mothers are allowed to give asylum for only a few short years and then they must stand back and watch, hoping for the best.

"I'm sorry, John," I said, and then added with my practiced enthusiasm, "I guess you'll just have to prove to Mr. Davis that you're *not* a spaceman."

"Yeah," he said, unconvinced. "I guess I will." He opened his binder and handed me a paper. "Homework note," he said. "I didn't finish coloring the map of Europe last night."

"You *didn't?*" I could make "You *didn't?*" sound worse than anybody else could ever make "Spaceman" sound.

"One of my lizards hadn't been eating and I was afraid he was sick, so I tried to make him eat, and then I cleaned out the cage and everything. And somehow the lid got knocked off the cricket cage and they all got out, so I had to spend an hour finding them, and I didn't get the map of Europe done. Can I go check on my lizard?"

"You know our agreement, John. If any homework is overdue, it gets attention *first*, before going out to play, before *anything*."

John sighed. "Anything except going to the bathroom."

"Right. Get to the map."

"Mom? Can I just go say hello to Jesse for a minute?" A quiver in John's voice made me turn and look at him. John had been one of the boys in a community production of *Oliver*, and I had thought he looked the perfect English waif, thin and pale and vulnerable. Sometimes I still see that waif in him, and at that moment I saw him, sweet and sad, holding out his empty bowl, "Please sir, could I have some more?" "Mom, can I just go say hello to Jesse for a minute?"

Oh, a child should not be so hungry. "Sure, John. Go say hello to Jesse."

The dog had seen John come home and had been leaping and scratching at the French doors that opened from the family room onto the back deck. As John stepped out, he was joyfully attacked by the big black animal wagging its tail and yelping in delight.

"Hi, Jesse!" Instantly John was loved and needed, knocked to the grass and licked on the ear. John laughed and wrestled the dog off him. "Wanna play catch, Jesse? Huh?"

Watching John resurrect to Jesse's dumb adoration, I recalled that first day he had brought the little, black, mostly Labrador dog home from the creek. "Please, Mom. He's been just wandering around up there for two days now. He needs a home."

"Oh, John. I don't know."

"Please. Please, Mom. I need a dog. I really need a dog. I think a dog would . . . would help me with stuff." John looked up at me with that empty bowl look, not contrived, sincere, haunting.

"Well, John. We'll see."

"Oh, thanks, Mom." The kids had learned that if they ever got me from "I don't know" to "We'll see," the rest was a piece of cake.

John had been right. He *did* need Jesse. And now as I looked out the kitchen window and watched the two of them fetch and throw and dig a ball out of the geraniums, I was grateful to this black dog that made John so happy, that simply delighted in him, that never asked him about homework or wondered what in the world was going to become of him. I was grateful to Jesse for being to John what his mother could not.

My frustration grew. How could John tell me so often in one day, "I forgot"? How could he have me deliver him to the church for a party that was being held the next day? How could he let me find in his desk at open house an unfinished Mother's Day card? How could he take twenty-five minutes to get dressed in the morning? (I passed by his door one morning, and ten minutes later I saw him in the same position, holding the same sock in the same hand. He looked at me, looked at the sock and shook his head. "I don't believe it either, Mom," he said.) How could he forget he had been assigned to give a talk in church as a youth speaker, remembering only when I, sitting with the choir, saw his name on the program, gestured to him frantically, and died a hundred deaths while he made a fair recovery and quickly put together a few extemporaneous thoughts on serving one another. How could he lose two math books and a binder and three coats in one season? ("The natural consequence to misplacing a coat is having to wear three old sweaters," said a book I was reading on childrearing. But any child would prefer pneumonia, so I came up with yet another coat.) Just before a trip to Utah I bought John some great sneakers at the thrift store for two dollars. While we were away I saw him wearing his old ones and asked if he had brought the new ones.

"No," he said evasively.

"Did you lose them?" I pressed.

"Well," he said, "what can you expect from cheap shoes? You pay two dollars for shoes . . . you lose them."

Somehow John charmed his way out of all his sins. Until junior high. I can hardly bear to even think about John and junior high. It would have to be high on my list of ten worst memories, and certainly one of the great black marks on my career as a mother. I began to yell. I cried. I punished. I praised. I bribed. I encouraged. I even swore a few times. I worked out systems of accountability. Nothing worked. I began to look at John as a different person. He was no longer just my dear and charming son. I still loved him and enjoyed him, but sometimes I found myself looking at him with a strange combination of anger and pity. Was John an incompetent? Was there something *wrong* with him? I mobilized the school's counseling office and had tests run. I made John's father come out from San Francisco for conferences with us. (Was *that* part of the problem? I had read that boys whose fathers are out of the home suffer in their schoolwork. But John's dreaminess had started long before Gerald left, long before John was three, in fact. He had brought the trait with him at birth, trailing clouds of daydream as he came. And Gerald, to the extent that he could, had always shown interest in John's schoolwork and encouraged him.) The counseling office assured us there was nothing wrong with John. He was just disorganized and unmotivated.

I found myself grasping every positive and negative motivation that came along. When I took the boys on a trip to New York City we saw a dirty and ragged young man of no more than thirty shuffling from phone booth to phone booth in Grand Central Station.

"What's he doing, Mom?" asked Aaron, wide-eyed.

"He's looking for change."

"How did he *get* like that?" asked John.

"He got bad grades," I said. *"That* is what happens to people who get bad grades."

I tried to remember which genius I had read about who had done poorly in school. Was it Einstein? But I knew that for every genius there were ten thousand failures shuffling the streets and checking phone booths for change. Could John end up as one of them? Could he someday be that lost, his clear eyes clouded, his hair unwashed and uncombed, a jacket from high school his only shield against the cold, or maybe a plastic garbage bag because he would have lost his jacket? Of course not. But . . . all those sad men, they hadn't all started out as failures. They had just dropped out or been pushed out or had fallen through the cracks somehow.

I felt John's entire future resting on my shoulders, and it was heavy. If he didn't care enough, or somehow couldn't do enough, I would have to do it for him. I would have to transfer my own energy to him, to make up for the energy he seemed to lack. The cargo that he carried was precious, but it would never be delivered anywhere if he couldn't get himself organized. I felt myself pulling him and pushing him like a workhorse brought in to get a wagon out of the mud.

The same conversation took place over and over again.

Me (patiently): John, I spoke to your science teacher on the phone today. He says there are five assignments that have not been turned in.

John (surprised): Really? Five?

Me: Yes, John. Five. How did that happen?

John (sincerely): I don't know.

Me: But the assignments are all listed on the wall of the room. Every day you can check to see what you have in and what grade you got. Didn't you know that?

John: Yeah. I guess so.

Me (evenly): Then why didn't you check the list on the wall?

John: I forgot.

Me (exploding): "I forgot!" That's your favorite phrase! John, you drive me crazy! What am I to do? Don't you *want* to do well in school?

John (quietly): Yes.

Me: Then why aren't you *doing* the simple things that need to be done, that anybody who has half a brain can do? John, you are a very bright boy. You have marvelous, marvelous gifts to give the world. But you'll never give them if you don't get on the ball. *What in the world is the matter with you?*

John (in tears): I don't know.

Me (yelling): Well, I'm sure I don't know either. And how do you suppose it makes *me* feel? How do you think I look traipsing down to school every week because my son can't get his act together? Well, I give up. I just give up!

But I didn't give up. John became a freshman, and I kept pushing and pulling and yelling and prodding and suffering. Suffering! It was a personal affront, a wound to my pride. I was failing as a mother. John was *making* me fail as a mother. My children had been sent to me as clay, hadn't they, and I was to mold them into something wonderful, wasn't I? What was I doing wrong? Every time I learned that a friend's child had been accepted at Stanford or received a scholarship to Brigham Young, a pain went through me. My children were not scholars. They were many wonderful things, but none of them spent long hours in libraries making sure their schoolwork was perfect. *I* had. Why wouldn't they? And how could John just drift along and see others leaving him behind in the dust?

Once again, yet once again, I sat John down in my room for another, yet *another* conversation. "John," I said solemnly, wearily, "high school is more important than you know. If you don't do well now, all your future options are limited. Did you know that UC-Berkeley rejects even straight-A students? Did you know it's getting harder and harder to get into BYU? I know you want to go to college. I know you don't want to spend your life pumping gas or something. And to do that you have to *make* yourself succeed. *I* have to make you make yourself succeed. I've drawn up a little contract here."

John sighed and turned away to face the wall.

"You're going to have to earn every privilege by performance in school—everything, weekend fun, television, friends over, everything. I know this sounds harsh, but do you know how harsh the world is out there, how competitive? Nobody's going to coddle you out there, John."

"Oh, Mom!" John swung around to face me and there were tears on his cheeks. "What you're doing isn't helping me. I know you're only trying to help me, but it *isn't helping*! Mom, did you know that a long time ago in Hawaii they had a big problem with snakes? The whole island was overrun with snakes. And so they brought in a lot of mongooses to get rid of the snakes. Only the mongooses killed all the birds instead."

Killed all the birds instead? Oh, John, I do not want to kill your birds! I have never wanted to kill your birds! Is that what I have been doing? I want those birds to fly, all those wonderful birds I have seen since the day you said, "If cows were clouds I would take my cup outside and fill it up and drink it down."

———

I tore up the contract. I backed off. I pulled my energy away and left John to his own. I tried not to care, not to panic when some of his grades were still pretty bad. I still yelled on a few occasions, still worried, but I tried more and more to watch for the birds and to admire them.

I no longer believe my children have been sent as clay for me to mold. Maybe they have been sent as clay for me to warm so that they can better mold themselves. Maybe, as Kahlil Gibran said, children have been sent not to us but through us. I am trying to look at John and the other children as people apart from me, who are not here to fulfill my plans for them but to discover their own best possible plan and to fulfill it.

Even Aaron, who will not read a book. He gets very good grades but will not pick up a book unless he has to. I beg him, bribe him, assign him, but he will not read. "I don't like to read," he said years ago, on a day when I was pushing for everyone to get a book and spend the evening by the fire reading.

"Well, what *do* you like to do?" I asked, disappointed and exasperated.

"I like to build things," he said in a small, sincere voice.

Of course. I knew that. I just kept finding it difficult to believe that anyone, especially a child of mine, would not rather read than just about anything else. Though it's hard, I'm trying not to judge that. Yesterday Aaron spent the entire day building a set of speakers for his stereo and he did a sensational job. I bought an electric saw for him and it wasn't even his brithday or Christmas or anything. But despite such efforts I will always remember that day, that one wonderful day when Aaron was reading a mystery I had finally succeeded in getting him into, and Katy came down from calling him to supper to report, "Aaron says to start without him; he wants to finish his book."

"I'll get him," said Emily, jumping up from her chair.

"No!" I grabbed her shoulders and pushed her back down, and whispered loudly, "Leave him alone. Don't anybody interrupt him for *anything! Aaron is reading!*"

———

John was able to qualify for the good-student discount when he got his driver's license, and he's happier, much happier, than when he and I were locked in combat over his schoolwork. He doesn't have the nervous habit of crossing and uncrossing his fingers that he had a few years ago.

But he is still forgetful and he probably always will be, even about wonderful things you'd think he'd want to remember. At eleven-thirty on a Saturday night a few months ago, he said sheepishly, "Mom, can we drive into San Francisco tomorrow?"

"Why?"

"Two of my paintings won prizes and they're giving out the awards in San Francisco tomorrow."

"Well, John, that's great! Why didn't you tell me sooner?"

"I forgot."

In February John sent his portfolio to the character-animation program at California Institute of the Arts in Valencia, and when the next month he was accepted (twenty out of sixty-eight were), I could not sleep for smiling.

Talk about hopeful! Talk about spellbound!

Oh, John, who cares if you can't do advanced math? Get a good calculator and hire someone to do your taxes. Who cares if you misplace your shoes? Marry a woman who can never find her purse. Just get enough left-brain support so that your right-brain gifts can be delivered—so that those wonderful birds can be kept in the air—and we'll all be thrilled.

2. Fourth-Prize Child

Katy, as the fourth child, usually got whatever was left at the bottom of the barrel. I was aware of it, but I didn't know whether or not she was. And I don't think she had that in mind the evening she said what she said to me, but it certainly made me think.

We were having a lovely evening together and I was kissing and hugging and tickling her. Suddenly I grabbed her and shook her and said, "Oh, Katy, Katy! How did I get *you?* I must have won the contest, and you were first prize!"

Katy shook her head seriously and said, "Oh, no, Mom. No. I was *fourth* prize!"

Fourth prize? Did she feel like fourth prize? I knew that Katy *wasn't* fourth prize, but I also knew, and felt terrible knowing, that Katy often *received* fourth prize.

There was the time Katy was busily taking only the chicken pieces from the dish of Chinese stir-fry I had served. "Katy, take some vegetables too," I said.

"I only want the chicken," she replied.

"Katy!" said John. "I don't care *what* Mr. Rogers says. You're not *that* special!"

We laughed, but now I have to ask myself was Katy special *enough*, and did she ever get her share of the chicken?

Once I overheard Katy in the kitchen say, "I think I'll have an ice cream cone."

Aaron replied, "Good luck, there's no ice cream."

"Oh. Then I'll just have the cone." And off she went, happily munching.

An empty cone? Is that what Katy had often been served?

I never meant it to be so, but Katy came at a difficult time. The other three came into a marriage and a family that was thriving. Katy came into a marriage and a family that was fighting for its life. She never saw animosity between her parents, but surely, surely she sensed the stress.

And Katy didn't have as much of her father as the other three had. He loved her, but he wasn't really there for her in the same way he had been for the others when they were small. He had taught Emily at age three to recite Juliet's famous balcony speech, but no such special moments were carved out for Katy. He wrote on her first birthday in a little diary that I kept for her, "Your arrival has been a sweet and revealing experience for me at a very difficult time in my life." However, the difficult time in her father's life came to absorb so much of his time and energy that only the leftovers were available for his children, especially the youngest. I watched him come and go and give what he could, and I knew that it was not enough but that nothing could be done. Did Katy, seeing Gerald spend four times as much time talking to Emily, just because they had four times as many things to talk about, feel indeed that she was fourth prize?

Not only was her father guilty but her mother too. I have far fewer pictures of Katy than I have of Emily, and far fewer tape recordings. Why did I let that happen? When time is divided and stress is multiplied, the last on the list loses out.

Katy's closet, of course, is filled with hand-me-downs. Going out to buy her brand-new clothes was not a common occurrence. Once Emily said to me, as she was campaigning for something she felt she needed, "Remember, Mom, the more you buy for me the less you'll have to buy for Katy."

When I noticed one evening that Katy had spent yet another dinnertime as a listener and not a speaker, I talked to the other children about it in private. "Sometimes can't you just *be quiet* and let Katy talk? I know you don't do it on purpose, but you guys almost never give her a chance to say much of anything."

"Mom's right," said Emily guiltily. "Poor Katy."

"Trying to get a word in edgewise with you three is like yelling above a jackhammer that never, never turns off. Sometimes just *listen*. Every day I want you each to ask Katy a question about school or something."

The kids were very agreeable, but also very forgetful. And Katy continued to receive less than her share of attention.

I had always been worried that Katy's light was being hidden under a bushel not of her own making. Was that the way it was for everyone who was the baby of the family? Emily and John and Aaron were so continually wired, so forever demanding the spotlight that it left Katy perpetually upstaged. She must feel absolutely overwhelmed, I thought to myself, as I watched Katy be an audience to the other children, a delighted audience, but an audience.

Why didn't she want to perform, even when we made a place

for her onstage and pushed her out? She is a beautiful child, with a finely etched profile, a lean and graceful body—she looks like a dancer, really. Yet it was difficult to get Katy to sing or to dance. Even in the car when she and I were alone and I suggested singing, sometimes she would, but more often she would not. Emily had been singing and dancing nonstop since she was two. Why wouldn't Katy? Or maybe . . . maybe that was the reason. Was the competition just too stiff?

And why did she have to dress in the most inconspicuous, dull clothing? Levis and a plain shirt was her standard uniform, and I got the feeling it was sort of like jungle camouflage. Anything that would call attention to her was refused. It became a challenge every Sunday to make her put on a dress for church, and then it had to look as little like a dress as possible. Anything ruffly or lacy or flowery or feminine was out, was "barfy."

One morning, to our great amazement, Katy came downstairs wearing a ruffly blouse and bright-figured pant set that she had refused to wear all year. She had even curled her hair.

"Oh, Katy," said Emily. "You look *so cute!*"

"Yeah," Katy said disdainfully as she lifted her nose in the air and bounced out the door. "It's *Nerd Day!*"

The fact that she found it difficult to express herself troubled me greatly. One night when Katy was about eight and she I were lying on my bed, I said to her, "Oh, Katy, tell me a story."

"You tell me a story," she responded.

"But I need a story. I never get a story. Tell me one. Make one up."

"I can't."

"All right, we'll make one up together. I'll start and you take up where I leave off."

"Okay."

"Once upon a time there was a wonderful . . ."

"Horse."

I waited. She was finished. I continued. "And this wonderful horse lived in a kingdom far away where the king of the land had a very big . . ."

"Problem."

Again I waited. Nothing. I continued the story for another minute. ". . . And the king decided he could never solve the problem because the problem was . . ."

Pause. "Big."

I laughed. "Katy, you're not playing fair. You're making me do all the work. Come on. So the *big* problem was that the king wanted . . ."

"A horse."

"What for?"

"To ride."

"Where?"

"Around."

I tickled Katy until she couldn't breathe. "Katy! You are no fun. Why won't you tell me a story? I need a story!"

"Oh, Mom," said Katy when she stopped laughing, "I am not a storyteller. I am a story *tellee.*"

Tellee? An eight-year-old who can come up with that is hiding an awful lot under her bushel. Did I do it to her? Or her father's absence? Or her overwhelming, intimidating jackhammer brothers and sister? Or is it just the way she is and there's absolutely nothing wrong with not wanting to sing or dance or tell stories or talk a lot or wear interesting clothing?

———

I think I always tried to make it up to Katy for being last and getting least. I nursed her forever. All the other kids had nursed longer than average, too, and then gave up when they were ready. Katy, however, asked to be nursed even past her third birthday. She wasn't relying on me for much physical nourishment; she was more of a social drinker. It was nice just to snuggle up to a warm body and be loved. One evening after she had been dealt one of life's little blows, Katy came and asked for a nursey.

"Oh, Katy," I said, "all right. Let's go in the family room and you can have a nursey while I read the newspaper."

"No," she said, "in the front room where the kids are watching television."

"But I want to read the newspaper, Katy."

"The right one in the family room," she said, "and the left one in the front room."

That was the last nursey Katy had. A kid that can do that kind of negotiating about a nursey shouldn't get one.

———

Katy certainly got a lot of love. Right off the bat she had all those adoring siblings, three more than Emily had, two more than John and one more than Aaron. The boys loved her, but Emily appropriated her. Katy was hers, the little sister she had longed for and prayed for and finally forgiven each boy in turn for not being.

Every once in a while Emily would look at Katy and shriek, "I'm having a Katy attack!" And she would run to Katy and devour her, hugging and kissing and leaving her limp and loved. Emily also had John attacks and Aaron attacks, but more frequent were her Katy attacks.

"Oh, Katy," Emily said one evening as the two of them rolled on the floor. "Don't ever leave me. I know what, Katy. Let's you and me marry Siamese twins so we can always be together!"

———

Why wasn't that enough? Why did Katy decide that she had to have a *puppy*?

I didn't need a puppy. I didn't need John's dog Jesse that he found at the creek. I didn't need the cat, the boa constrictor, the turtles, the lizards, the hamsters, even the goldfish. But it was clear to me that other people in the house needed them.

The first time Katy said to me, "Mom? You know what I want,

what I really, really want?" I was paying my usual half attention.

"A horse," I guessed. That was safe. Both of us knew it was the impossible dream.

"Nope. A puppy."

"Oh? Really?"

"Please."

"Katy, you're kidding. We already have a dog."

"But he's not mine. I need a puppy, my own puppy."

I'd better nip this in the bud, I thought, and turned to her with my full attention. "Katy, there is not a chance in the world, not one tiny little itty-bitty chance that we are going to get another dog. I'm sorry. End of story."

That evening before supper I walked by Katy's bedroom door and saw her lying on her bed crying. I went in and knelt down beside her. "Katy! What's the matter?"

"My puppy. I want a puppy so bad." Her delicate features were squeezed toward the center of her little face as she turned toward the wall and sobbed.

I sighed. This morning the washing machine had broken. This afternoon I read one of *my* poems in Ann Landers's column, credited to Author Unknown. I had just learned that a friend's mother died. And now Katy needed a puppy.

I took her in my arms. "Oh, Katy, Katy, I'm sorry. We can't. We just can't."

"Why?"

And so for the first of maybe seventy-four times I went through the list. We already *have* a dog. I could not deal with having another dog. She would want her dog in the house and I had not been able to stand the smell and the fleas when Jesse was allowed in. Puppies pooh and wet all over the house. What if Jesse and the puppy did not get along? Her cat Juliet would hate having a puppy here. I can hardly bear one dog's barking; how could I bear two? And the money, shots, food, veterinarian bills. "Katy, it is impossible. There are things *I* would love to have, but I can't have everything I want. No one can. I'm sorry."

The next day she brought it up again. And the next day. And the day after that. I would hear the front door slam at 4:10 and think about hiding in the bathroom. She would bring it up playfully and bring it up in tears. She would tease and she would beg. She would make jokes and she would give reasoned arguments. She would bring it up *every day*.

On the grocery list I keep on the wall in the kitchen I found in a handwriting not my own, "Puppy for Katy."

On my list of things to do, fastened to a clipboard on my desk, I found in the same handwriting, "Get puppy for Katy."

Once she left on my bed a Shel Silverstein book, open to the verse

> . . . And Abigail began to cry and said,
> "If I don't get that pony I'll die."
> And her parents said, "You won't die.
> No child ever died yet from not getting a pony."
> And Abigail felt so bad
> That when they got home she went to bed,
> And she couldn't sleep,
> And her heart was broken,
> And she DID die—
> All because of a pony
> That her parents wouldn't buy.
>
> (This a good story
> To read to your folks
> When they won't buy
> You something you want.)

She discussed the dilemma with our friend Lynn Ann and took her advice to just let me think about it and not mention it for three whole weeks. That didn't work, however, as I thought Katy had given up and I was overjoyed.

When the barrage began again, I got what I thought was a fine idea. "Katy, my dear," I said enthusiastically, "I think I've got the answer. How about if Jesse becomes *your* dog? John is agreeable. You know Jesse doesn't get the attention he deserves. We'll take him down to The Little Lamb and have him bathed and clipped and he'll come home with a nice ribbon around his neck and smelling good, and we'll have an adoption ceremony here, and you can even give him a new name if you want to and he'll be *Katy's dog*." My voice had been growing more and more enthusiastic like when I used to talk about how much fun it would be to go to the dentist and get a balloon and a brand-new toothbrush. "How does *that* sound, Katy?"

Another hand-me-down? Katy was quiet for a moment, and then looked at me sadly and sincerely and shook her head. "That's not exactly what I had in mind, Mom. Jesse's okay for a big, black dog, but he's not my puppy."

Well, I had tried.

It was madness born of desperation, I'm sure, that made me agree to take her runt hamster to the vet two mornings before Christmas when she discovered its tiny leg had been chewed off, and *pay thirty-six dollars* for a suture and an antibiotic. I was amazed as I watched myself writing the check. But if the poor girl was not going to get a puppy, I could at least take her runt hamster to the vet.

It didn't work. Nothing would satisfy but a puppy. I avoided Katy. I reasoned with her. I put my foot down and demanded I never hear the word puppy again. I felt alternately like a rotten mother who would not sacrifice for her child and a browbeaten captive who was being tortured and used. But I would not give in.

One afternoon I came home later than I'd planned, and she ran to the door excitedly to meet me. "Where've you been?"

"I went for a walk with Annie," I said. "And then I stopped for a few groceries. Why?"

"Oh. I thought that maybe . . . you were out getting my puppy."

The straws were getting very, very heavy on the back of my determination. The last one fluttered down on Sunday afternoon when Emily, who had found herself processing some unexpected unresolved feelings about her father's death, sat us all down for a serious meeting. She wanted to make sure that none of the other children were stuffing feelings about him that should be dealt with, and she quizzed each of them in turn.

AARON: I'm okay. I figure when something bad happens you don't just sit around and worry about it. You get up and go on from there.

JOHN: I don't think about it very much. I'm not hiding any feelings, I don't think. It just happened, and it was too bad, but I'm not carrying it around with me.

KATY: Well, about once a day I sit down and cry about the things that I can't have—like my daddy and a puppy.

Ping! I felt the straw land and heard the break begin. There was no way out. No way out.

"Well, Katy," I said to her that night, "I think we ought to move you downstairs into the guest room."

"Why?"

"It'll probably be more convenient to have you train your puppy down there."

Katy shrieked and jumped and nearly knocked me over. "*My puppy?* Oh, Mom! Oh, thank you, thank you, thank you!"

On the way to bed I began to generate a little enthusiasm. Sure. Why shouldn't Katy have a puppy? Even if it was just one more thing for me to deal with, even if I actually had to pay money for it, didn't Katy deserve, just once in her life, to get first prize and not fourth? To have not a hand-me-down, but her very own, brand new, top-of-the-line, world-class puppy?

I researched the best breeds for a family pet, took Lynn Ann's suggestion of a keeshond, learned from a friend of a litter just born in Utah, talked with the owners long-distance, and arranged with a friend who was flying back to bring the puppy on the airplane. My excitement was building. *My* excitement to add yet one more pet to this household was *building*.

And Katy's was off the chart.

Driving to the Oakland airport to pick up the puppy was almost as thrilling as going to the hospital to get a new baby, and it didn't hurt at all. All my labor pains had come in delivering the idea, but after the idea had been born breathing I was okay. The sight of the bay with its sailboats always made me smile, but I found I was smiling before we even spotted the water. I may yet feel some guilt at slighting my fourth child, but always, always I will have the bright memory of that first-prize day, of Katy at the airline counter swooning with delight as she opened the little wire door of the carrier out of which poked the nose of Bridget Baby Brown Eyes.

———

Yesterday two wonderful things happened. Well, three, actually. Ann Landers called to apologize and told me she would run a special note giving me credit for my poem.

But better, Katy and I took our first tap dancing class together, and she *loved* it. Katy is a dancer after all, not a dancee, but a dancer! (Though she's insisting we take the ribbons off her tap shoes.)

And best, I held out to her a wishbone that had been drying on the breadbox for days. "Make a wish, Katy," I said.

She thought a moment, then giggled. "Mom," she said, "I can't think of a thing to wish for. Not a thing!"

3. Not *My* Son!

Once I had a dream that Aaron died. All I can remember of it now are huge rocks and a twisted bicycle and Aaron lying in my arms lifeless, cold, and pale. And the terrible, huge sadness that sucked me back into consciousness. I gasped in relief to feel my bed under me and to hear the grinding of the neighbor's lawnmower. My fingers went to my eyes and felt tears.

I got up quickly and threw on my bathrobe. I had to find him, had to see him move. As I opened the door of his room I saw that it was empty. I hurried down the stairs and into the kitchen. There at the bar sat ten-year-old Aaron, eating raisin bran, chewing with his mouth open, as usual.

"Oh, Aaron!" I put my arms around his shoulders and dropped my face onto his neck.

"Huh?"

"I dreamed you were dead. It was awful!"

"Hmmm. Sorry."

I was still crying. "Aaron, come sit with me for a minute."

"I'm eating."

"Come sit with me, Aaron." I walked to the couch and reluctantly Aaron followed, letting me pull his upper body across my lap and cradle him as I had in the dream. I stroked his face and it was warm. I put my hands over his lips and felt breath. He was alive.

I did not look at that dream as a warning, though I have since cut out and left on Aaron's plate newspaper accounts of all the bicycle and motorcycle accidents I can find. I looked at the dream as my private dramatization of how dear Aaron is to me. Sometimes I need to be reminded.

Aaron is my daredevil, my prankster, my questioner of authority, my rough and sometimes rude one. He is the one who dives first off the tallest cliff into Lake Powell and laughs to shame the more cowardly. He was the one who always played with matches despite every early lecture and threat and who was the wonder of the neighborhood boys as he built little bonfires in the middle of the cul-de-sac on which we lived. He was the first of the children to go to the emergency room of the hospital, taken there at age three after he had pushed a pussywillow up his nose because it felt interesting. He is the one who spreads a layer of salt inside Emily's sandwich even when it's not April Fool's Day. He is the one who I knew was being referred to on the several occasions that a school office called saying there was a problem with a child of mine.

Such as the incident in fifth grade.

I was outside sweeping the front walk when Aaron rode up on his bicycle.

"Mom," he called out before he even put on the brakes, "you know what happened at school?"

"What?" Day after day I asked Aaron that question and the answer was always, "Nothing." It must have been something big.

"My classroom got vandalized. Over the weekend somebody broke into Mrs. Latimer's room and tore up a lot of papers and books and threw the desks around and poured glue and shellac and stuff everywhere, and they left a big knife sticking out of Mrs. Latimer's desk."

"Oh, Aaron! That makes me so mad!" I imagined Mrs. Latimer walking into the room she had arranged so carefully and leaning against the door frame as she looked around in amazed sadness. The very picture made me moan. "Who would have done such a thing?"

"I dunno."

"Well, it just makes me furious! Mrs. Latimer is a wonderful teacher. How dare somebody do that to her room? Do they know who did it?"

"Nope." Aaron popped down the kickstand on his bike and went into the house. I continued sweeping, filled with an energy that came from anger. If I had my hands on the kid who would do a thing like that, I would kick him around the block.

———

The next day as I was down at the school going from room to room helping judge the science fair, I ran into Mrs. Latimer.

"Gee, I was sorry to hear about your room," I said. "Is there anything we can do to help?"

"Thanks," she said, shaking her head. "Uh . . . has the principal spoken to you?"

"To me? No. Why?"

"He thinks . . . that it may have been Aaron and Steve."

A cold rush filled my body as I stared at her, unmoving. "Aaron? And . . . ?"

"And Steve." She looked as if she was in pain to see my pain.

After a moment I spoke. "Do *you* think that Aaron . . . ?" I could not even complete the thought.

"I would be surprised," she said slowly. "Aaron's a terrible showoff, but I've never seen him do anything mean. I . . . I don't know. The police have been here all day. They're checking. Mr. Roland thinks . . . You'd better talk to him."

Hardly able to make my legs move, I walked to the office. "Is Mr. Roland in?" I asked hesitantly.

"Oh, hi," said the secretary brightly, looking up from her desk. "No, he had to go somewhere with the police officer. He'll be in first thing tomorrow."

Did she know? I wondered. Would she speak to me that brightly if she knew that the principal thought my son had vandalized the classroom?

I hurried to the car. Aaron would be home in an hour. I would wait for him, just wait for him and then get this whole thing cleared up. Aaron wouldn't lie to me. He hadn't lied about the bomb he had built out of match heads and flash powder and set off in a field and scared himself half to death. He had *done* it, but he hadn't lied about it. Aaron would tell me.

I sat down in the reclining chair and tried to meditate. "Shalom . . . shalom . . ." My mantra kept faltering from the sound and sight of a knife sticking out of Mrs. Latimer's desk, still dancing from the thrust of a young hand. "Shalom . . . shalom . . . whose hand? . . . whose hand?"

"Mom?" Aaron's voice screamed at me from the front porch. His bicycle clattered to the sidewalk and I heard his feet take the stairs two at a time. I took a deep breath and pushed the recliner upright.

"Mom?" He burst into the room, face white and eyes flashing.

"Hi, Aaron." I tried to stay as calm as my mantra.

"He thinks I did it," Aaron shouted. "Mr. Roland thinks *I* vandalized the classroom, me and Steve!"

"I know. I was down at school today. Sit down, Aaron."

He sat on the floor, back against the gray couch. I looked at him for a moment and he looked back. "Aaron?" I asked quietly. "Did you do it?"

"No!" He rose to his knees in outrage, then settled back down, wiping an arm across his eyes. "Of course I didn't do it!"

"What happened today?"

"Just after school started, Mr. Roland comes in and takes Steve out of class. Then about an hour later he comes back in and he says, 'Aaron Pearson?' and he motions me to come on out, like this. So I go, and he puts his hand on my neck and leads me toward the office and he says, 'You know why I'm bringing you here, don't you?' And I couldn't figure out what he was talking about, and I said, 'No.' And he said, 'Oh, come on, you know what's going on, now don't you?' And when we got to his office, there were two policemen. Brother King—you know, the policeman who goes to our church—was one of them. And then I figured it out, and I thought, 'Oh, crap, they think I did it!' And then they read me something about like I have the right to keep silent . . .' Aaron's voice broke and he pushed it harder to keep the story going. '. . . and do I want a lawyer? And I must have given the wrong answer because he said, 'So you do want a lawyer?' And I said no, and he said, 'Will you answer our questions?' And I said yes. So they started asking me all these questions about where I was on Friday night and who I was with."

Friday night. He was home, of course. And he was with . . .

"So I told them I was with Steve. He stayed over here on Friday night and then we went to the A's game the next morning. Steve must have told them the same thing, that he spent Friday night at my house."

That was right. Steve had spent the night here. They had played around outside until maybe ten, but then they had come in.

"You didn't . . . go anywhere with Steve Friday night, did you, Aaron?"

"Just up to the creek."

"And then you went to bed."

"Yeah."

"And you were here all night, weren't you?"

Aaron's eyes rolled in disgust, then he spoke in the pseudopatient tone he had probably learned from his mother. "Yes, we were . . . here . . . all . . . night."

"Okay. So that's why they brought you in, because Steve had told them you were together. But why did they bring Steve in in the first place?"

"I don't know. Something about his shoes. Mr. Roland said Steve and I were the two he would pick out of the whole class anyway who might think up something like this and then when he found out that we were together on Friday night. . . ." Aaron slumped down and kicked his backpack across the room.

I was quite for a moment. "Aaron? Why did the principal say you and Steve were the two he would pick out?"

" 'Cause he doesn't like us. He thinks we're troublemakers."

"Are you?"

"Just little things. No big things. He busted me once for riding my bike where it's restricted, but I was really just pushing it but it looked like I was riding it, so he busted me. And in the lunchroom Steve and I got busted twice for talking too loud, but we weren't talking louder than anybody else. And Mr. Roland says I talk back, but they don't want to hear what you have to say, they only want to hear what they have to say. It's messed!"

"Aaron, being a principal is a tough job, like being a parent is a tough job. Nobody does it perfectly. But I think Mr. Roland is a very good principal, and he does a lot for the school and for you kids."

"He's messed! And he thinks I did it, and he told the police he thinks I did it!" Aaron face was twisted and angry.

"One problem is this, Aaron," I said. "You got yourself a reputation for being someone who pushes the rules to the very limit. And so when this kind of thing happens, yours is a name that comes to mind. I'm sorry."

"Well, it's messed! And it makes me mad!"

———

The next morning I went down to school and opened the door to the office.

"Good morning." Was the secretary's voice less bright than it had been yesterday? Did she know? Did all the teachers know? Did half the students and now their parents know that Aaron Pearson was a suspect in the vandalism?

I sat down across from Mr. Roland, his desk between us. He tried his best for the friendly, easy manner he was known for. But it wasn't quite as friendly or as easy as I remembered it. Earlier in the year I had sat there with my four children as we all sang for him the school song I had been asked to write. The song was nice and the children were charming and everybody was impressed. That day he had looked at me and seen a respectable, helpful, contributing member of the school team. But today? I could sense it. Today he saw me as the single mother of a delinquent child. The Pearsons were no longer a charming family, but a broken home. And Aaron, the product of a broken home, was a vandal. Steve lived in a single-parent home too. Of course. Of course two boys without fathers, living with overworked mothers who can't control their children, are the likely suspects. What do you expect?

"The police think they're on to something," said Mr. Roland, leaning back in his chair and looking at me evenly.

"What do you mean?"

"They got some good footprints. There were two sets of shoes, one larger than the other. Tennis shoes like most kids wear. The larger shoe had a pattern that's exactly like the sole of Steve's shoe. Same size, too. In fact, the police took Steve's shoes into custody this morning. His mother had to bring down another pair for him to wear. The smaller shoe was harder to get a clear print of. But Steve's shoes look like pretty firm evidence. And if Steve and Aaron were together on Friday night. . . ." He didn't want to say it and I didn't want to hear it.

"Aaron told me he was not involved," I said slowly. "Aaron has never lied to me."

Mr. Roland shrugged his shoulders. "I'm sorry. You might want to visit with the police officer assigned to follow through on this. I understand you know him. Officer King."

"Yes. I know him."

———

Officer King was out for the rest of the day, but he could see me at ten o'clock the next morning. I tried to write, placing five blank white pages beside the typewriter to inspire me, but it didn't work. My mind had a life of its own that day. Was it possible, was it remotely possible? Mothers who work at a bank or at a grocery store can keep on working when their kids are in trouble. The work is right there and they just do it. Mothers who stay at home and try to write can't. If their kids are in trouble, the page stays blank. I got up and cleaned all three bathrooms. A mother can always clean bathrooms.

Aaron came in from school as cheerful as usual and headed to the kitchen to make a peanut butter sandwich. "Mom? I'm going over to Lee's house till supper. Okay?"

"In a minute, Aaron. Tell me about Steve's shoes."

"What about them?"

"The police took them. They have the exact same design on the sole as the footprints in Mrs. Latimer's room. And they're the same size."

"So? Hundreds of shoes must be. Steve didn't do it. He was with me."

"What do the soles of your shoes look like?" I tried to sound curious but not suspicious.

"I dunno." Aaron lifted up a foot and looked at the bottom of the shoe. I quickly memorized the tiny waffle pattern covering the sole.

"Mr. Roland says the police think Steve's shoes mean something."

"That's their problem." Aaron and his sandwich were out the door.

I snuck into Aaron's room and shut the door before the other children saw me. Besides Aaron's church shoes there was only one other pair in the closet, ragged shoes he mostly wore at the creek, and the pattern of the sole was X's and O's as in a massive game of tic-tac-toe. What in the world was I doing in there looking at Aaron's other shoes? Didn't I trust my own son? I looked around at the half-open drawers and the desk piled high with a twelve-year-old's treasures and the dirty clothes in and around the laundry basket. Did this room belong to someone I did not know, someone who could look me in the face and lie to me, someone who could sneak out of the house in the middle of the night and destroy his teacher's room and leave a knife sticking out of her desk? Of course not. Aaron was sometimes foolish, but not mean. He had looked in amazement at the crutches chained to the grillwork in front of the apartment in New York City as a bicycle might be chained. Somebody would steal crutches? No, Aaron was not mean.

But did we ever really know anybody else, even our own

children? What about all those statements of surprise from family and neighbors when some young person was caught in a terrible crime? "He was such a nice boy. I never dreamed he could do such a thing." A parade of criminals passed through my mind and a parade of their mothers, women who could not hold up their heads, women who had to live the rest of their lives with the knowledge that their child had done a dreadful, dreadful thing. How could they bear it? How could *I* bear it?

I picked up Aaron's baseball mitt, touched his scout scarf, looked around at the shell necklace, the piece of stained glass, the screwdrivers and pieces of things mechanical, the toy horse with rider, the posters of Boston and Van Halen and the postcard of Garfield saying "Hello From the Funny Farm." Was this the room of a criminal? Of course not. But every kid who does something wrong is just a kid with his own stuff in his own room and his own mother who loves him. We would have to sort this out and do whatever we could do about it.

Emily caught me coming out of Aaron's room. "Hi, Mom. Whatcha doin'?"

I sat in her doorway and watched her take off her sweater and put away her school things. "Emily? Do you think there's any chance, any chance in the whole world that Aaron was involved in that vandalism?"

"Nope." She didn't even pause to think. "Aaron is pretty dumb sometimes. But not that dumb."

———

Mothers can't sleep either, when their children are in trouble. At least not for a long time and not very well. When it's dark and you're tired, and especially when you have no one there to share the concern, terrible images stand between you and sleep. Of course Aaron didn't do it. Why couldn't I simply dismiss it? Aaron would never do something like that. Besides, he didn't act guilty. He couldn't fool me. I had a master's degree in drama and

I knew he was not that good an actor. And he had always come clean right away about even the stupidest things he had done.

In third grade he had come home from school and kissed me and I had nearly fallen over from his tobacco breath.

"Aaron! Tell me about the cigarettes!"

"Oh," he said sheepishly. "How did you know? On the way home I went into Gary's house for a minute and there were some cigarette butts in the ashtray and we played smoking."

"Did you light them?"

"No. We just chewed on the butts."

"Aaron! How disgusting! Do you want to do it again?"

"No, it was yucky."

"Well, please don't. You smell terrible. Go brush your teeth."

And just last month his whole scout troop had gotten in trouble for having a six-pack of beer in the tent. When I confronted him he admitted that he had taken a sip.

"I'm sorry, Mom," he said. "The older guys brought it out, and I remembered what you had told me, that sometime that was going to happen and I'd better know what to do, and what I should do was just to run, to get out of there. And I tried to think how I could do that. Only it was dark and leaving our tent was not allowed, so I couldn't run. I sat in the corner for a long time, but then they made me feel so dumb. So I took just one sip, and it didn't even taste good."

Oh, Aaron! But he had not lied.

———

As I drove down to the police station I tried to decide if I should say, "Officer King" or "Brother King" like I do at church. And would he call me "Sister" or "Mrs."? Of all the policemen on the force in Walnut Creek, why did the one assigned to his case have to be someone we *knew*? Why couldn't this be done anonymously? And who else would know by now? Even before I had completed the thought I was ashamed of it. He wouldn't say a word to anyone. Of course he wouldn't. He probably hadn't even told his own wife.

Walking up the steps and into the police station felt surrealistic. I didn't belong here. I had never walked into a police station in my life except to license a bicycle. Other mothers came to police stations to talk about their kids, sad mothers from ghettos with bad children. But not me.

"Have a chair, Sister Pearson." Brother King smiled, his clear blue eyes looking at me warmly, not accusingly. Then he indicated the box of Kleenex on the edge of the desk. "Sometimes people need that." The only other places I had seen boxes of Kleenex left out were funeral homes.

"This is a brand new experience for me," I said. "What a mess. The school principal told me about the shoes and I wanted to get everything straight from you. What do you think?"

"About who did it? Well . . ." He pulled from a drawer a paper with the outline of a shoe on it. "This is the first footprint, the one that matches the shoes that we took into custody, Steve's shoes, with these snakelike squiggles running from toe to heel. And the other set . . ." He reached again into the drawer. "The other was a smaller shoe, sort of a waffle design."

My heart hammered and I held my breath while he pulled out the other paper, a shoe print with waffles—large, *very large* waffles. "That's not Aaron's shoe," I said.

"Aaron's? No, it isn't. I made sure I got a good look at Aaron's shoe sole when we had him in the principal's office."

"And his old shoes aren't like that either."

"I have no reason to suspect Aaron. That first day when we questioned him I didn't get the feeling that he was hiding anything. You learn to read people pretty well when you're a police officer. I didn't think Steve was lying either, but these shoes are a problem—same design, same size. I don't know what to make of that. And then with the two boys being together that night . . . it was just an unfortunate set of circumstances. But I'm sure Aaron was not involved."

"I am too," I said, and I reached for a Kleenex.

———

The following week Aaron burst in the door with a big grin on his face. "Mom? Good news! The Christian Academy was vandalized last night!"

"Oh? Well, that *is* good news. I've been hoping that would happen."

"No, Mom. There were the same two footprints, the one that matches Steve's shoe, only they know it can't be Steve because *his* shoes are still locked up at the police station! So good old Mr. Roland can't blame me and Steve anymore. Great, huh?"

———

And so that was the end of the incident in fifth grade. Except for the following month when the school secretary called to tell me someone had scratched a bad word on the principal's door and they thought it was Aaron, and I asked Aaron if he had done it and he looked me in the eye and said yes. He watched me cry for a few minutes and told me he was sorry and listened to my lecture about how he had let someone who thought he was a vandal turn him into one. He said again that he was sorry and he promised me that would be the last thing like that he would ever do in his whole life.

———

Aaron's character has improved considerably since fifth grade and I feel his checkered past is behind him. He's been getting all A's and B's in school. He got 100 percent on his road test, something the instructor hadn't seen in a long time. He performed a fine classical guitar solo from Bach in church recently. He played the lead last spring in *Mame*, the school's musical. He's well on his way to being an Eagle Scout. I learned that the other day he and a friend took flowers to a girl they know whose boyfriend broke her heart. He volunteered to go with John's church group to work in a soup kitchen in San Francisco when several boys couldn't make it. He's a junior in high school now and not *once* has the school office called to tell me that he's in trouble. In short, I think there's reason to hope that Aaron will grow up to be an outstanding citizen.

Of course, there were the brownies. I did not take it very well when I learned that a few months ago Aaron and Mike had put Ex-Lax in the brownies that they had taken to a Sunday school party and several people had been up in the night with diarrhea. I did not take it well at all. And when I learned that the bishop had asked Aaron to come in for a visit and it wasn't even time for his six-month interview, I was chagrined.

"So how did it go?" I asked when he returned.

"Don't worry about it, Mom. The bishop told me *he* put Ex-Lax in the brownies once, only he was in college and he got busted by the dean. He just told me to keep the lid on it. Night, Mom. Love you."

4. The "L" Word

Why can I remember, nineteen years later, the exact day and time and even what I was wearing and where I was sitting? This was no monumental occasion like the death of President Kennedy, which I heard about in an elevator in Moscow, Russia, from a Canadian hockey player who was very tall and wore a navy sports jacket and a red tie. This occasion was absurdly commonplace. Why have I remembered it so vividly?

Marda and I were propped up on my big waterbed with our first babies. We were not close friends but knew each other from church and had brand new motherhood in common. She had been out strolling in the crisp November air and had dropped in for a visit. Emily, about five months, was lying on the bed beside me in a green knit jumpsuit with yellow embroidered flowers, and Kristen, about four months, was contentedly reclining in a baby carrier near her, sucking a small rattle. We were chatting about the usual things new mothers talk about, sleeping through the night and breast-feeding, when all of a sudden Marda grinned and lunged at her baby and exclaimed, "Oh, Kristen, I love you! I love you, I love you!"

A strange combination of feelings washed over me. First a wave of embarrassment and maybe a little disdain. How gushy! How silly to be so emotional, and in front of someone else, too. Another wave quickly followed. Envy. Envy! Oh, how would it feel to be so uninhibited and warm and overflowing and maybe even gushy? How would it *feel*?

After Marda and her stroller crunched down the sidewalk over the dry brown leaves, I sat down in the front room of our small student apartment and stared out the window, Emily at my breast and a strange sensation at my throat. I was not a good mother. I would never be a good mother. Here Emily was five months old and I had never told her that I loved her.

I had hardly ever told anybody, "I love you." I seemed to have almost as hard a time saying the word "love" as the other four-letter words I had been taught to stay away from. I had told Gerald, my husband, that I loved him. I had said it honestly and with meaning, but the words had never, ever sprung uninhibited from emotional overflow. When they came they came, like most things in my life, from my left brain, not my right; they came as an expression of fact.

It wasn't my fault, I reasoned, if indeed this is a fault. I had never learned how to be affectionate. People are what they grow up with. I had grown up in a safe but emotionally sterile environment, and here I was, crippled, just like the Chinese girls whose tiny feet had the bindings finally unwound.

My mother and father tried their best to make a good family. They had married late in life and it wasn't until my mother was thirty-nine that they had their first children: twins. Three more followed. Were they too old to find marriage and parenthood fun? Or were they just by nature very sober people? They planned well and gave us everything their means and skills allowed. But some things come only unplanned, come only from spontaneous emotional overflow. I knew that my parents loved me. But I never *felt* that my parents loved me. And I never heard the words. If ever my mother had gushed, "Oh, Carol Lynn, I love you, I love you, I love you!" it was when I was too young to remember. And I don't remember my parents ever saying the words to each other. Well, perhaps they just didn't say them in front of us.

But what kind of an excuse is that? Did the sins of the fathers *have* to be visited upon the children? Did this sweet little person at my breast have to grow up emotionally undernourished just because *I* had? Life had always been serious business to me. Nowhere was there joyful, spontaneous overflow, on the inside or on the outside, and later when I observed it in other people, I must have stared like a tourist at Niagara Falls. During my growing-up years, every once in a while a friend or a complete stranger would startle me by asking why I looked so sad. I didn't feel sad, I just felt normal. Still, that was why I tore up the yearbook picture. I was in eighth grade. My art class came directly after the yearbook class, and one day as I took my seat I noticed that one of the pictures had fallen to the floor unnoticed. I picked it up. It was *my* picture, me—a little girl in a polka-dot blouse, looking so sad, so sad I could hardly bear it. Her hair was funny, her face had pimples, and her eyes were *so sad*! Was that me? That person didn't deserve to be in a yearbook. Glancing around to make sure nobody saw me, I put the picture in my pocket. Later that night at home I tore it up, and that year my face did not appear in the yearbook.

Life was not unremittingly grim. I got straight A's. I achieved. I won contests in speech and writing. I was in all the plays. I was fairly witty and I could make people laugh. Witty—but not warm. My passion found expression in performing and on the page and in an intense desire to travel and to make something of myself, but always one step back from the frightening arena of real life and human relationships. I had been told that I had a reputation for being stuck-up and that hurt. I didn't feel stuck-up. I just felt inadequate. How I envied people who bubbled, who overflowed, who looked like they loved themselves and everybody else. I would try to figure out how they got that way, but I could not begin to explain it or imitate it.

And now with a baby at my breast I felt hugely, hugely inadequate. Emily deserved better than me. She deserved a mother who could shower her with love, who could warm her day and night, who could say the words without even thinking about it.

Emily finished her nursing and lay back on my arm like a little drunk, eyes closed and pink mouth open, a drop of milk slipping down her chin. I lifted her up and kissed her forehead. I had kissed her a lot, caressed her a lot, massaged her a lot. That counted, didn't it? I had read Ashley Montague's book about touching and how really important it is. I had talked to her and read poetry to her, inside and outside the womb. So what if I had never told her I loved her? Emily would just have to take what she got, and what she got was me. I could only be what I was.

Then it occurred to me. Emily didn't *know* what I was. She didn't know that I was not a warm and emotionally responsive person. Nobody had told her that I was stuck-up. She had no idea that I was insecure and inadequate or that I had torn up my yearbook picture in eighth grade. I didn't have to be that for her. Maybe it wasn't exactly like the Chinese girl's bound feet. Maybe I could start all over again! Emily would accept me any way she found me.

"Emily? Hey, wake up, you sweet little creature." I said it as a term of endearment. I had never called anybody "darling" or "sweetheart" or "honey," in my whole life, not even Gerald. I called him "kid," or "luv" and he knew it meant "darling." But "darling" was a word my lips would not form. It was too direct. Could I say it to Emily? Nobody was around. She wouldn't laugh. "Dar . . ." It didn't sound right. "Sweetheart." That didn't sound bad. It sounded kind of nice. "Sweetheart. Emily, Sweetheart." I kissed her forehead and her cheek and her closed eyes and her pink little mouth. "Did you know I love you, Emily? I love you, Emily. Sweetheart, I love you."

By some great marvel, Emily turned out to be the child that could always say it. As soon as she learned the words "I love you," they were hers. And she gave them away over and over, throwing them in the air like bright confetti or rice at a wedding. This gift she got from her father, to whom warmth and overflow came effortlessly.

By the time Emily was about six, she had established a pattern. After the bedtime ritual was complete, she would say to each of us, "Good night. I love you." We would, of course, reply, "Good night, Emily. I love you too." And then, if she happened to get up for a drink of water or to go to the bathroom or to tell us something she had forgotten, we would go through the ritual again.

"Good night, Daddy. Love you."

"Good night, Em. Love you too."

"Good night, Mommy. Love you."

"Love you too, Emily. Good night."

The repetition might occur several times before she was finally asleep. And if, for whatever reason, one of us merely said, "Good night" without adding the "Love you," Emily would repeat her statement, underlined, until we responded the right way. Only then would she be satisfied.

One night when Gerald and I were cleaning the kitchen

together, after the ritual had taken place three times, he stopped scrubbing the frying pan and turned to me. "Blossom, what about this thing with Emily? She forces us to say 'I love you' half a dozen times a night. Sometimes I don't feel *loved*, I feel *manipulated*."

I laughed. "It's her security blanket, I think, or her teddy bear. She just can't go to sleep without it."

The next night Gerald tested her. He gave her one perfectly good "good night" with lots of love, shown and spoken, and then put her in bed. Half an hour later, as he passed her open door, she called out, "Daddy? Are you going to bed now?"

"In a minute."

"Night, Daddy. Love you."

"Night, Emily." He continued down the hall and into our bedroom.

"Love you, Daddy," called out Emily.

"Good night, Sweetheart."

In a minute we heard Emily's bare feet padding down the hall and she appeared in our doorway, little butterflies on her nightgown and important business on her mind. "Good night, Daddy. *Love you.*"

Gerald smiled and held out his arms. "Emily, Emily, Emily. What is this? I told you tonight that I love you. You know that I love you. Why do you have to *make* people say it again and again? Sometimes I feel like a rubber ball you're playing with."

Emily's lip quivered. "I just have to."

"Why?"

"Last year in kindergarten we saw that movie about fire safety, and a house burned down and killed everybody in the family."

"I remember. You were pretty scared."

"And I decided that if our house ever burned down in the night and we all died, I wanted the last thing I ever said to anybody to be that I loved them, and I wanted the last thing anybody ever said to me to be that they loved me."

"Oh."

"And I can't go to sleep if we haven't done that."

"Hmmm. Well, in that case, Emily, good night. I love you." He kissed her and Emily smiled.

"Good night, Daddy. Love you too."

————

Saying the words had become easy with practice, like learning a new language. It was not like a stunted foot with the bindings removed. *Some* growth was possible, and I watched it in myself, a student of Gerald and Emily, with as much reverence as I watched the growing of the rose bushes in spring. I finally could talk about this with my brothers and sister, and as adults we have become good friends. We've each found ways to adapt and grow and we've become late bloomers. But it has not been easy and it has not been complete, and each of us still bears some scars from those early years. Sometimes my siblings and I have watched my children interact and we've envied them and learned from them, and I have watched my sister Marie and her daughter Cherene together and wished that we had had such warmth between us and our parents. All five of us say "I love you" to one another now, quite belatedly and not as easily as my children do, but we say it.

Even my father learned some things late in life. I have to tell you that getting an emotional response from him was about as hard as getting cool weather for the Fourth of July parade. I saw him get really angry a time or two, like when somebody parked blocking our driveway one Sunday; I don't think I'd ever seen him that angry. He showed approval, too, when it was called for. But not affection. Once I came across some love poems he had written to my mother when they were courting, and I was astonished. They were as sentimental as you please. Why did none of that ever show in real life? Why do I remember seeing only a few pecks hello and good-bye between them, nothing playful, nothing warm? Why do I have only one memory of my father sitting on the couch with his arm around my mother, and that on the day she came home from the hospital to spend a little time with us on the Christmas before she died? How I wish I could remember love and fun and warmth there. It would have changed my life, I know.

  When I finally figured out that now that I was all grown up it was as much my responsibility as my father's to mold the relationship, I tried. I said the words to him. The first time was on paper. In the year I spent abroad I wrote him regularly. It's easy to sign a letter, "Love." That doesn't really mean much. But as I sat alone for a whole day on the shores of the Sea of Galilee, I made a lot of resolves and one of them was to be a better daughter. My mother had died long before, and I figured we'd just take up sometime where we left off when we could; but my father was here, and I had to do something now. I wrote a long letter to him. It took hours, in fact, and threw me into a kind of a stage fright, so that my fingers were damp and the pen kept slipping. I expressed appreciation for all he had done for me, and I actually wrote: "I love you, Daddy." It wasn't easy, but it was easier way over on the shores of the Sea of Galilee than in the same room. I knew he wouldn't open the letter for at least five days.

A strange thing happened in my father's last years. He mellowed a lot. He talked about some things he'd never talked about before. And he even told his children that he loved us, all of us, and we talked about it and were impressed. The best story about his transformation is the one Aunt Cree told me.

I liked to drive now and then from Provo to Midway to visit Aunt Cree and Uncle Karl. Especially in the autumn when the aspens turn yellow and the oaks turn red, the drive through the canyon is breathtaking. Aunt Cree was Daddy's little sister and I knew he liked her a lot. When we visited there when I was a child he used to open her door without knocking, something I could not even believe, though she never seemed to mind. I liked Aunt Cree. She was the wise old woman of the farm, ample, intelligent, generous, who told wonderful stories and bottled shelves of marvelous things like apple butter and raspberry jam.

One day I began to quiz her about the family my father grew up in, thinking it might shed some light on the family he created. I learned what I'd suspected: Daddy's parents practiced a kind of pioneer emotional austerity. The marriage was solid but not particularly warm, and Aunt Cree remembered a few months when their parents did not live together and nobody knew why. It appeared that Daddy was a product of his home, just as I was a product of mine, and he could only give me what he had to give.

"But you know something?" Aunt Cree asked, as we sat together on the bright crocheted afghan that covered her couch. "Your dad has been doing some changing. Something real unusual happened a couple of months ago when he was out here. I was sitting right here where I am now, and your dad was sitting over there across the room, and we were visiting, you know, I don't remember what about. And all of a sudden he said to me, 'Well, Cree, I don't believe I've ever told you that I love you, have I?' And I said, 'Well, no, I don't believe you have.' And your dad stood up and walked clear across the room and gave me a hug and he said, 'Well, Cree, I love you.' Now, can you beat that?"

I liked that story. I told it as I spoke at Daddy's funeral. It means that bindings are not the end of the story. That last week when Daddy was at my home just before he died, we both said the words a number of times. It was never as easy to say them to my father as to my children, but that very fact at least speaks well for the progress of generations. And I was glad my children had some time with their grandfather. Especially Emily.

"Do you want a drink of water, Grandpa?"

"No, thanks, Emily." If he'd been feeling better, he would have called her Hoptoad, as he often had. Hoptoad. His best term of endearment.

"Good night, Grandpa. Hope you feel better. I love you, Grandpa."

"Good night, Emily. I love you too."

Oh, I was so glad he got to hear love from one who spoke it so well, who knew it as a native tongue, not as a second language. So glad.

———

How lucky I have been. In all the years, the good years and the bad years, especially some rather recent years when the eyes I saw in the mirror were so sad I would have torn up the glass if I could, I have had Emily to say the words, say them for all of us and to all of us. I am the mother, but Emily has been the leader, orchestrating the family affection, and I am only grateful.

"Good night, Mom. Love you."

"Good night, Em. Love you too."

"Good night, John. Love you."

"Love you too, Em. Good night."

"Good night, Aaron. Love you."

"Night, Em. Love you too."

"Good night, Katy. Love you, sweetheart."

"Night, Emily. Love you too."

If Emily has to come into my room for something after I've gone to bed, she still has to say it again. And I say it again too, and I don't mind at all. It is possible that the house might burn down that night. And it was, of course, the last thing she said to her father as he lay dying on the living room couch and I held the telephone receiver to his ear. "Good-bye," she said, "Good-bye,

I love you." It made a title for a book I wrote about Gerald and me, but better, it made Emily's father smile his final smile.

I've learned a lot from my good little teacher. I figured I might finally get a passing grade the day Katy came home from school and said, "Mom? Our teacher made us all tell today what things our mothers do that embarrass us the most."

"Oh, no," I braced myself. "What did you say? When I sing in front of your friends?"

"Worse."

"When I do my yoga exercises out by the car while I'm waiting for you at school?"

Katy shook her head. "I said that the thing my mother does that embarrasses me the most is that sometimes like when we're in an airport or something she grabs me by the shoulders and shakes me and says real loud, 'Oh, Katy, I love you! Do you hear me, do you hear me?' "

I broke into a laugh. "You're kidding! *That* is the most embarrassing thing I do?"

Katy put her hands on her hips and stared at me indignantly. "Yes!"

I grabbed her and shook her and told her that I loved her.

Emily is away at college. I didn't say she could go. As she was putting the last of her things in the cardboard boxes and the suitcases, I told her no, it was not allowed, she was to unpack immediately. But she went anyway.

I'm going to call her on the phone tonight, and she will say it.

I'm going to listen down the hall tonight as the other children get ready for bed and I will hear my gruff teenage Aaron say "Night, Katy. Love you." And Katy will reply, "Night, Aaron. Love you too."

I'm going to leave up on my wall, where I can see them from

my computer, several of the many little notes I've received over the years. One drawn with hearts, "I love you, Mom." Another, "Mom, have a wonderful trip. And remember I love you with all my heart." And, "Hey, sexy lady, will you please leave by the door a check to pay for my gym suit and put my clothes into the dryer before you go to bed? Love you, Mom. XOXOXO, Emily." I'm going to leave them up there until they're yellow and they fall in little pieces on the floor.

5. Our Friendly Neighborhood Obscene Phone Caller

When the phone rang I was expecting a call from the library on a book I'd asked about.

"Hello?"

"Would you like to f——?"

I slammed down the receiver and felt my blood pump and drain like it does when you're almost in a car accident. My hand still clasped the receiver tightly and I could feel the heavy pulse in my fingers.

What? Why? How dare he? This is my home, *my* home! An intruder had entered and slapped me across the face and I couldn't even see him!

The phone rang again and I jumped. I pulled my shaking hand back and stared at the telephone as if deep examination would reveal the caller. Finally I reached out and picked up the receiver, one hand poised to cut off the call.

"Hello?" I said tentatively.

"Mrs. Pearson? We do have the book and it's in. Shall I hold it at the desk?"

"Oh. Yes. Thank you."

I tried to go back to my writing, but I couldn't. Strange, unwelcome words kept appearing between my eyes and the page. How dare he? He had ruined my whole morning. How *dare* he? I had received only one other obscene phone call in my life and that was about ten years ago. Oh, well. I suppose I could bear such a thing every ten years.

———

That night I heard Emily answer the phone and then say, surprised, " 'Scuse me?" She slammed down the receiver.

"What was that?" I asked suspiciously.

"Some jerk."

"What did he say?"

"You don't want to know."

"Yes, I do."

"He said, 'Do you want to you-know-what.' "

"He called this morning."

"He did? What a jerk."

Emily bounced back to her homework and I sat down on the couch, troubled. One phone call could be a mistake, a random happening, but two in one day was alarming. He was not just dialing a random series of numbers that happened to be ours. He was dialing *our number*. Why? Before I went to bed that night I unplugged the telephone. That was dumb. What if there was an emergency and somebody needed me? Well, they could do without me. I needed to feel safe for a while.

Why did I find this so troubling? Lots of people received obscene phone calls all the time, I supposed, and didn't let it be any big deal. Why was it a big deal to me? Why had I always found obscenity or vulgarity so repulsive? When the children started bringing home colorful words from school or the neighborhood my standard response was, "You can throw that word away, please. It's a garbage word and I don't ever want to hear it in this house again." For some reason the first two months we were in our new home all kinds of garbage words appeared. Once I carried out the threat of washing out a mouth with soap. And once when I learned that Aaron had tried out some newly acquired language on a little girl who had run home crying, he and I walked up to the girl's home and had a meeting with her and her father, in which Aaron apologized and promised never to say such things again.

I even react to mildly offensive language, and the kids know it. One afternoon Emily came home from high school and fell giggling onto the couch.

"What's so funny?" I asked.

"I can't tell you Mom. It's too gross," she managed to say.

"Well, if it's that funny maybe I can handle it."

Emily tried to compose herself. "We were reading in my English class today, taking turns reading out loud. And this boy—he's not a very good reader—it was his turn, and he made a terrible mistake. He was supposed to read, 'And so Harold stuck a carnation in his buttonhole and went to the party.' But instead of 'buttonhole' he said . . ." Emily collapsed again.

"Never mind," I said. "I get the picture."

Actually, I laughed at that one—it was pretty funny—but usually I do not laugh at butt talk. One day when I felt the kids were getting a little too gross, I said, "Enough. I have had it, do you understand? No more butt talk."

"*But, Mom!*" Emily exclaimed, and all four children hooted with laughter.

So okay. I can handle butt talk. Sometimes. And I've gotten

used to a few other words I would not personally choose. But not the real stuff, the heavy stuff, the stuff obscene phone calls are made of and and thrown at an innocent person in such a cowardly way. And now I had been violated twice in twelve hours.

Next morning just before nine, I was sitting down to start writing when the phone rang.

"Hello?"

"Would you like to f——?" It was the same soft male voice.

I slammed down the phone and stood up, furious and shaking. How dare he? What gave him the right to reach into my home and throw his garbage at me? What a jerk. What a damn jerk. Damn was about as bad a word as I ever used and mostly I just used it in my mind. Well, maybe he would get tired of calling. I was doing the right thing. I was just hanging up. I knew you weren't supposed to respond to an obscene caller or yell at him. He'd get tired of calling.

He didn't. Once or twice a day or maybe every other day he called. He became an anticipated nuisance, annoyance, enemy. Emily found him stupid; I found him scary. We named him the Jerk. When the boys or Katy answered the phone, he hung up without speaking. But when Emily or I answered, he delivered his message, always the same soft voice, the same words, not the least variation. Poor dumb jerk has no imagination, I thought. I found myself constantly on guard, sometimes laying bets with myself every time the phone rang, sometimes when it was him being quick enough to cut him off before he finished his short message. He was supposed to get bored with this and quit. Why wasn't he?

"Emily," I said one evening, "I think it's probably somebody at your high school. He doesn't call during school hours, and he sounds pretty immature. Can you think of anybody it might be?"

"Mmmm. No."

"Are there any boys at your school that look or act strange?"

"Mom, *most* boys at my school look *and* act strange!"

———

How had teenage pranks degenerated to this? When I was growing up in Provo, Utah, the really daring, outrageous kids might every once in a while pick up the telephone and dial the local grocery store.

"Do you have pop in a bottle?" they would ask.

"Yes, we do," would come the response.

"Well, you'd better let him out. Mom wants him home for supper." They would slam down the telephone and squeal and roar.

And once when an incredibly witty boy was over at my house and the phone rang, he picked it up and said, "Mormon temple. Angel Moroni speaking."

I'm sure the person who answered the telephone at the grocery store got plenty fed up with calls about pop in a bottle, but I had been drafted into a whole different ball game. There was nothing fun about it. Had the years moved us into a darker era? What was the Jerk getting out of this? It was chilling.

The first time he called in the middle of the night I was furious. And frightened. What kind of a person was this? He never threatened, never said anything about *doing* anything. But I began to worry. In the middle of the night the mind gets pretty creative. Did he know where we lived? Was he watching us? Did he look at Emily and Katy as they came home from school? Did he know I was a single woman, that there was no man in the house? Damn him! *Who was he?*

Next day I called the phone company. Their response was just what I'd expected, which was why I hadn't called before. Obscene phone calls happen all the time, I was told by the woman in the nuisance-calls office, and only rarely can the phone company put a tap on a phone. Her first suggestion was that I change my number and give the new one only to those I trusted. I'd already thought of that, but I didn't want to do it, to contact a huge list of friends and business acquaintances and to tell the children to guard the new number carefully. And if the caller knew who we were he could find a way to get a new number. I was not going to live my life in hiding; I'd rather do battle openly. The woman then suggested that I keep a log of the calls to see if a pattern emerged, which would show me exactly what I was dealing with and might help identify the caller. That made sense.

When I hung up, I went to the calendar and made note of the call from the night before. "The Jerk 2:30 A.M." I also marked in the two previous calls.

What else could I do? If it was somebody around here, I reasoned, maybe other women were receiving the calls too. I started canvassing the neighborhood just like I do in the annual Mother's March for the March of Dimes. Only this time it was less pleasant.

"Hi. I have a real strange question for you. Are you, by any chance, receiving obscene phone calls?"

Bingo. Two were. Two women who lived near me had been receiving them regularly for about as long as I had. Same message.

"A call usually comes as soon as my husband's car leaves the driveway," said Rena. "It makes me so angry!"

"The phone rings as soon as I walk in the house," said Joyce. "Sometimes I just know it's him, but what can I do?"

So there were three of us, and who knows how many others? My gosh, the poor Jerk was a busy man. He had to hustle right home from school or work or whatever and get right to his phone calls. Imagine the time and the energy going into that. Poor Jerk!

It had to be one of the teenage boys in the area. It had to be. I knew that improved our chances of identifying him, but it saddened me too. It was probably someone we knew. I mentally listed the five teenage boys I was aware of. Who could it be? Joel? I'd given him rides home from school when he and Emily had stayed late for play rehearsal. Tom? Richard? They sometimes stayed up late at night to study the stars through their telescope. Jack? He was a pleasant, athletic boy on the football team. Kyle? I knew him least but liked his polite, friendly manner.

That night I quizzed John and Aaron. I had not made a big deal out of this for them, as I wanted the children to feel more secure than I did, but I thought now they might be helpful. "You know those calls we've been getting, Emily and me? From the Jerk. I think it's probably someone in the neighborhood. Who do you think it might be?"

"What exactly does he say?" asked John.

For the first time I repeated the Jerk's message to the boys.

Aaron laughed. "Oh, that's Jack!"

"How do you know?"

"We were all over at Dan's house one time and Jack went to their phone and dialed a number and said that exact thing."

Jack? Jack, the good-looking tall blond boy with the quick smile? Jack, who made sure his two little sisters didn't have to walk home alone in the dark when they played at our house and stayed too late? Jack, who'd cheerfully helped me when I'd interrupted a ball game out on the street to ask for volunteers to distribute flyers regarding a neighborhood event? My own boys had whined, "Oh, Mom!" But Jack had taken the whole stack, given some to each boy and sent them off. "Come on, you guys," he'd said. "It won't take long." Jack was the Jerk? I didn't want it to be Jack. And his mother was such a nice woman; one of her daughters was Katy's age and we had been "room mothers" at their school together once.

I dreaded the next call, not sure what I was going to do. But a week passed and there were no calls. School had been out for a month now and the calls had come in the daytime as well as the evening, but now they had stopped. My hopes rose. Maybe it was over!

After the week of silence, however, two mornings in a row brought 10:30 phone calls. I said nothing, just hung up as usual. Did I dare speak to him? Was I right that it was Jack? Did I have enough evidence to really be sure?

That evening I ran into Jack's mother at the grocery store. "Oh, it's good to be back," she said.

"You were gone?"

"For a week. We went to the beach. Left on Sunday and got back on Sunday."

The last calls I'd received before that were Friday and Saturday. And they'd started again the day after they had returned from the beach. There was no more doubt: Jack was the Jerk. I prepared in my mind a little speech for the next time he called, and rehearsed it over and over again, dreading the moment. I didn't have to wait long. The next morning at 10:30 the phone rang.

"Hello?"

That same soft voice. "Would you like to f—?"

"Jack," I said slowly and clearly, speaking to him for the first time in seven months, "this is the last call of this kind you are going to make. If ever I get another one, or if any other woman in our neighborhood gets one, I'm going to your parents with proof of what you're doing. I never want to hear from you again."

Shaking, I put down the receiver. If I'd somehow been mistaken and it wasn't Jack, the caller would probably phone again just to show me. I waited. Nothing happened. With some satisfaction, I imagined the shock on the poor kid's face when he heard me speak his name. For the next two days I held my breath each time the phone rang, and each time I felt relief when it wasn't him. We had been liberated. The siege was over.

Weeks passed. I asked Rena and Joyce if their calls had

stopped, and they said yes. I told them what I'd done, without revealing Jack's name. Why did I feel such an urge to protect him? Why did I watch him come and go on his bicycle (avoiding my eyes, of course) with a kind of compassion, maybe even responsibility? A very odd bond seemed to have developed between us. We'd shared an intimacy for seven months, a negative one of course, but an intimacy nonetheless. I couldn't put him to rest. The poor Jerk. Anyone who devoted so much time to something so destructive had to be deeply troubled. What was it? The phone calls were only symptomatic. Jack needed help. How could I walk away from him? No child is just "yours" or "mine." We're all in this thing together. If one of my children had a problem that I didn't know about and someone else did, I would want her to tell me. Even it if hurt, I would want to know.

I called the police department and asked to speak to someone experienced in dealing with obscene calls.

"Why does a boy *do* things like that?" I asked the sergeant.

"Puberty. He's probably experiencing some powerful sexual urges and for some reason is acting them out through these calls."

"Would I be right to tell his parents about this?"

"Absolutely. The boy needs help to redirect his energies, needs counseling. His parents have to see that he gets it."

One day after school had started and I knew Jack wouldn't be home, I did what was even harder to do than sitting down to start a new book. After avoiding it for as long as I could by cleaning up the kitchen and sweeping and putting new paper towels on the roller and trying to talk myself into minding my own business, I went to the telephone and called Jack's mother.

"Sharon? Carol Lynn. I need to talk to you. Can I come over for a few minutes?"

"Sure," she said. "Come on over."

There. That was the hardest part, like writing the first paragraph of a new book. The walk up the hill left me breathless; I wanted to get this over with, now. Sharon let me in and I complimented her on the new carpet and drapes, stalling like an insecure swimmer on the high dive. Then I jumped in.

"Sharon, there's something I need to talk to you about. It's about Jack."

"Jack?"

"I think he's been involved in making obscene phone calls, and I felt you should know."

Then the whole story poured out: that other women had been receiving them, that my son had heard Jack make one, that their vacation had coincided with the week of no calls, and that the calls had stopped altogether when I'd spoken to the caller using Jack's name. "I didn't want to tell you this, Sharon," I went on, seeing the shocked expression in her eyes, "but if Jack needs help, you're the only one who can get it for him. I'm sorry."

"I'm . . . I'm glad you told me," Sharon said slowly, staring at the new carpet. "Jack's a good boy."

"I know he is."

"He's under such a lot of pressure. His stepfather is determined to make a real man out of him, and now. If he gets below a B in school there's hell to pay. He's given a long list of chores every day and they're never done quite well enough to please Dave. He made him mow the lawn three times on Saturday so that he missed going to the beach with his friends. He's always onto him. If they're in the same room together Jack can't relax. He never relaxes until Dave's gone to work and then when he gets back Jack's all tense again. He even started to stutter this year. He's never done that before."

We talked for two hours. We looked in the phone book and found a local mental health agency that offered help. A counselor advised Sharon on how to approach her son and warned her what not to do.

"I'm grateful you came," Sharon said as I left. "I really am."

"Let me know how it goes, will you?"

It was not only the downhill slant that made the walk home much, much easier.

We spoke a couple of weeks later. Sharon and her husband had confronted Jack. Jack denied it at first, then began to cry and admitted he'd made the calls. They'd had a couple of sessions with a family counselor and Sharon felt hopeful that they could begin now to work on some things.

For the next two years I watched Jack come and go on his bicycle, still not looking at me. But I looked at him and was ready to smile and once in a while I even said hi. They've moved away now, and I pass by where they used to live and send Jack a good thought.

I looked at my own children too, and still do, and wonder what things each will do to offend. I don't expect any of them to make obscene phone calls, but they have each done some things to make me cover my eyes. Emily scratched a neighbor's car when she and her friends soaped it down in the middle of the night. John broke the window of a car at whose tires he was throwing rocks. You've already read a long list of Aaron's pranks. Just yesterday Katy got in trouble with the bus driver for spitting paper balls out the window—but she's still just a kid. Please forgive them. They're mine and they're yours and yours are mine too. And we're all in this thing together.

6. Peace on Earth Begins with the Mother

Once Katy said to me dreamily, "Mom, do you know when the happiest time of my life was?"

"When, Katy?"

"The week I got to go to horse camp."

"Really?"

"Yep. And do you know when the second happiest time of my life was?"

"When?"

"That week that Aaron was gone to scout camp."

Katy and Aaron are always bumping up against each other.

———

"Katy, will you move over?" Once again it seemed terribly important to these two that their elbows not touch while sitting at the kitchen bar for supper.

"No! *You* move over!"

"Look! Look at all that space you've got. Look! From right there clear over to . . ."

"Aaron, come on," I begged.

"There! Look how much space she's taking, Mom! Her elbow's practically in my food!"

"Good! Move!"

Aaron's elbow smashed into Katy's elbow, and Katy's elbow smashed into her plate of spaghetti.

"Now look what you've done," she screamed, as the plate crashed to the floor and the worms of spaghetti slithered over the linoleum.

"It's all your fault," laughed Aaron. Aaron finds everything amusing, at least everything that he instigates.

"That's enough!" I exploded. "How can we ever have world peace until we can have peace in the Pearson home? How can we expect Russia and America to get along until Aaron and Katy can get along?"

"Oh, Mom," said John, "you say the dumbest things. Like Aaron and Katy are going to affect the whole international scene and cause World War Three or something!"

"That's not so dumb as you think. In the meantime, you two just march out to the garage for a summit conference and don't you come back in until you've got a plan for peace."

"Hey, Mom," said John, "maybe you ought to send Reagan and Gorbachev out to the garage and make them come up with a plan for peace."

"You bet," I said, giving the two offenders a small push in the right direction. "That's exactly what I ought to do!"

In a few minutes, Aaron and Katy bounced back into the kitchen, friends again.

"Well?" I demanded.

"We have decided," said Katy, folding her arms across her red sweatshirt and making the pronouncement like a little judge, "that whoever sets the bar should put my yellow plate and Aaron's blue plate at opposite ends so that we don't have to sit by each other."

"Okay. Now all you have to do is figure out how to keep the peace when you're not eating."

Some months later, the Soviet poet Yevgeny Yevtushenko was completing a twenty-three-city tour of the United States, with a final stop in Berkeley. I had admired him for years and so I went to hear him.

At dinner the next evening I said, "Chew quietly, Aaron. I'm going to tell you all about last night and I don't want you to miss a word. Mr. Yevtushenko was *wonderful*! He is a giant of a man, very dramatic, throws his whole body into his reading, has a deep, passionate voice. He read in Russian and in English. *And* he asked me to give you guys a message."

"Huh?" Aaron grunted.

What Mr. Yevtushenko actually had said was this. Pausing in his reading, he stepped closer to the packed audience and said, "And now I must tell you something I am not proud of. This is a sad thing to tell you, but I must. I have been divorced three times. I have just married for a fourth time. I am not proud of this. It is not good. And I have come to see something that is very important. I want the whole world to live in peace. I want America and Russia to live in peace. I want there to be one big, peaceful, global, human family. But I have come to see that we can never have that big, wonderful family until we can succeed in our little families. This we *must* do."

That is what he actually said. But just as he used a translator for some of his poems, I did a little translating for my children.

"Mr. Yevtushenko said to tell you guys, 'How in the world can we ever have world peace until we can have peace in the Pearson home? How can we expect Russia and America to get along until Aaron and Katy can get along? And until Mrs. Pearson can find a better way than yelling at her children?"

Katy stared at me, amazed. "He said that?"

I nodded. "Yep, he surely did."

———

I was not just making it up that my children's quarrels affect the universe. I'm convicted that a web of energy connects every living thing. Plants flourish if they're emotionally nourished and wither if they're verbally abused. And I even believe the report that I read (no, not in the *National Enquirer*, in the *San Francisco Chronicle*) that a large group of meditators targeting a city back East succeeded for several months in affecting the crime rate, the suicide rate, and even the weather. Why not? We're all in this thing together. *My* job is to make my tiny unit (me) and my larger unit (my family) contribute harmony and not disharmony to the whole. The only hard thing about that is that it's hard.

———

The theory is perfect—until you open the floor to discussion.

"So what do I do if some kid comes up to me at recess and picks a fight?" asked John. "Just let him cream me?"

"Huh *uh!*" responded Aaron. "Anybody messes with me is going to get it."

"Tough man!" said Emily.

"Now, think about this," I said. "Aaron wants an eye for an eye and a tooth for a tooth, but people like Jesus and Gandhi thought we should return good for evil."

"Oh, right Mom," said Aaron, laughing. "If somebody steals my lunch I'm supposed to run after him and say, 'Wait, wait, you forgot to take my milk money!'"

The kids all broke up at that, and even the mother did, but I was not about to abandon my lecture. "Hey, I know it sounds strange," I said, "maybe even ridiculous. But if we could *get* to that point, if enough people could get to that point, we could change the world! The easy thing is to strike back, to . . ."

"Well, Mom, I know what you're saying," interrupted John, "but really, tell me, *when* can I hit somebody back? I mean, I'll never hit somebody first, but when can I hit *back*?"

There was no easy answer. Do we ever hit back? Do we ever go to war? While touring the capitol building in Washington I had been very moved to read on the statue of Jeanette Rankin of Montana, the only legislator who voted against entering World War II, "I cannot vote for war." And yet, what would have happened if we had stayed out?

All we can do in our own corner of the world is to try, even though doing the right thing isn't easy. Even figuring out what the right thing is can be really hard.

The case of the stick of gum is a good example. Emily was maybe nine, John was seven, and Aaron six. Just after supper a neighbor boy came over and gave John and Aaron each a stick of gum.

Emily saw this and immediately accosted the boys. "Let me have half, Aaron. Can I have half your stick of gum? Please!"

"Oh, all right." Aaron opened his gum and looked at it for a moment, then popped the whole thing into his mouth.

"Aaron!" Emily squealed.

"I changed my mind," he said, and walked off.

Emily dissolved into angry tears and came running into the house and told on him.

"You're right, Emily," I tried to comfort her. "That was a rotten thing to do."

"Aaron's a bum. I hate him."

I pulled out a piece of gum from a hidden trove and handed it to her. "Here, Em. Sorry. Aaron is just a little boy who is still learning how to be nice."

"He's *never* nice! I'm going to get him back."

Emily studied the silver-wrapped stick of gum in her hand, then marched toward the door and out onto the front porch. "*This'll* show him," she said. "Aaron! *Aaron!*"

Aaron looked up from pumping the tire on his bicycle. "Yeah?"

"Mom gave me a stick of gum."

"So?"

"Do you want half?"

Aaron eyed her suspiciously and took a half step toward her. "What'd you do to it?"

"Nothing!" said Emily in her most righteous voice. "It's perfectly good gum."

"Huh uh. You put something on it."

"Did not." Emily smiled and held out the gum for Aaron to examine and unwrap. "I am returning good for evil, because you are a bum!"

Aaron looked at her blankly, tore the gum in two, and put half in his mouth as Emily turned on her heel and flounced back into the house. Good for evil? Well, gum is gum.

You have to start somewhere, and maybe doing the right thing for the wrong reason—to show your brother—is the place. I'm never quite sure of my own motivation, being only a few years older than Emily, but I do the best I can for my age.

———

It was New Year's morning, several years later, when we discovered that someone had stolen the bulbs out of all the

Christmas lights that John and Aaron had so carefully hung around the outside of the house. A few broken bulbs lay on the sidewalk in splintered circles of red or yellow or blue, but the rest were simply gone.

"Oh, that makes me mad," said Emily, now thirteen and outraged. "It was one of the boys in the neighborhood. I just know it was!"

"Well, they're gone," I said sadly, "and I doubt very much if we'll ever find out where they went." It made me angry, too. The lights had been a luxury. Every other house in the neighborhood had long strings of colored lights that blinked their good cheer from mid-December on. "Our house looks so sad, Mom. Can't we get lights?" the kids had begged. It had not broken the bank to get them, but I had considered the lights a significant purchase. Maybe by next Christmas I'd feel rich enough to buy another eight dozen bulbs.

Emily turned and hurried indignantly down the walk. "I'm gong to find out who took them and I'm going to get them back!"

"How?" I asked.

"I'll find Glen," she called back. "He knows *everything!*"

"I'm going too!" Aaron ran after Emily and I watched the two of them hurry up the court, determined detectives. It was chilly but sunny, a typical winter day in Northern California. I had never gotten used to a holiday season without snow. You have to work harder here than in Utah to make things seem like Christmas. There'd be no mistaking the holiday season there, even without colored lights on the house.

I felt sad as I went about my morning work. This was not a good way to start the new year. This was the season for giving, not for taking, for basking in goodwill, not for having to remember that in the middle of the night on New Year's Eve some inside-out Santa Claus came along and stole your lights.

Within an hour I heard the door slam and Aaron call out, "She got them! She got them!"

Hurrying to the porch, I saw Emily triumphantly marching down the court holding a large brown bag.

"You should have seen her, Mom. It was so *rad!*"

Rad? There was no time to ask for definitions.

John and Katy raced down the stairs to hear the news. "Who did it? Who took them?"

"Kent did. Glen said so. And Emily went right to his house and banged on the door and Kent's mother answered. Oh, it was so rad! Emily said, 'Kent stole our Christmas lights and I want to see him right now.' His mother just about like dropped her teeth and she called him out of his room, and his dad came out too, and she asked Kent if he took our Christmas lights. He looked scared to death and said no, he didn't. So Emily walked right up and yelled in his face, 'You stole our lights and they must be in your bedroom right now, and I'm not going home until you give them back to me!' Kent's face went like all red, and he went into his bedroom and brought out this sack, and his parents apologized all over the place, *and if there are any missing he has to pay for some new ones.*" Aaron's face glowed with admiration. "Emily was *so rad!*"

Triumphantly, Emily put the brown bag down on the porch and began to lift out the colored bulbs like long-lost jewels. "He liked to throw them against concrete and see them smash," she said in great disdain. Then she smiled. "But Kent is in *big trouble* now!"

The other children laughed and began the process of getting the bulbs back into the fixtures. All day they made jokes about Kent, how dumb he was and how Emily had really nailed him. During supper I answered the doorbell, and there stood a shamefaced Kent, holding a sack with several new packages of colored bulbs in it. He thrust it at me, eyes focused intently on the mailbox, and said, "Sorry." Then he turned and hurried away.

By Sunday night the kids had forgotten all about the incident, but I continued to be troubled. Somehow it didn't seem . . . finished. It hung in my mind like dirty dishes that had been stuck in a cupboard and not washed.

That evening I sat the children down and said, "I've been thinking about Kent today, and what we're supposed to do to those who treat us badly."

"Oh, no!" shrieked Emily, throwing a pillow on the floor and falling on top of it. "I'm not going to love Kent. Don't make me barf!"

"We're not finished with him yet."

"*I'm* finished with him. I don't ever want to see his stupid face again!"

"We can't be finished until we return good for evil."

The kids began to laugh. "Marry him, Emily," giggled Katy. Emily grabbed her around the neck in a mock strangulation, while the boys whooped.

"Kent doesn't deserve good," Emily said. "Not only does he steal our Christmas lights but he goes around telling everyone at school that I'm in love with him. He doesn't deserve anything good."

"Nobody said to return good for evil if the person deserves it," I interrupted. "That's none of our business. We just have to *do* it."

"Do what?" asked Katy suspiciously.

"Well, that's what we need to talk about. What can we do for Kent?"

"You mean *to* Kent," insisted Emily, punching the pillow.

"Like . . . like do something *nice* or something?" asked Aaron incredulously.

I nodded.

"You're crazy," said Emily. "This is the dumbest thing I've ever heard of."

John was intrigued. "Hey, wait. We could get him a present out of our surprise-gift fund."

"No way!" said Emily. "That's for people who have problems and we want to help them."

John was getting enthusiastic now. "Kent stole our lights; of *course* he has a problem. I say we get him a present and sneak it up there and he'll never know where it came from. In fact, it'll probably drive him *crazy!*"

Oh, no. Love your enemies . . . it'll drive them crazy. Had our State Department ever thought of that?

Eventually the kids agreed. We took out five dollars from the little ceramic owl bank and gave it to John to go down to Thrifty's the next day and select something.

The following evening all four children helped wrap the sticks of colored clay that John had bought and wrote a note that said, "To Kent, from some people who love you." Emily had scratched out "love" and written "like," but we wrote it over again. As soon as it was dark they all ran out of the house, telling each other to be quiet, and five minutes later ran back giggling.

"Great going, kids," I told them. "That was definitely rad!"

Whatever that means.

———

I didn't see or hear much of Kent for the next several years, but only recently, during the holiday season, coincidentally, something quite wonderful happened. The phone rang, and when I answered it, a pleasant voice said, "Mrs. Pearson? This is Kent from up on Camino Verde. I was wondering . . . I work at the library now, and they're getting rid of some old books, and I picked up this rhyming dictionary and I remembered that you were a writer and I thought you might like to have it. It's only got one page missing, and if you want it I'll run it by."

"Well, gee, thanks Kent. That's very nice of you. I'd love to have it."

Kent stood on the front porch and proudly held out the book to me. "It's only got one page missing," he said.

I invited him in and we sat by the lighted Christmas tree for a few minutes and I asked him how he was doing. Just fine, he said, starting college soon, learning that life requires some serious commitment, planning to be an electrical engineer, working hard.

I smiled the whole rest of the afternoon. What a nice thing for Kent to do. I mean, it was *really, really* rad!

It's easier to love the kid up the block sometimes than it is to love your own. And it's definitely easier to love the Ethiopians, for whom you can stick a check in an envelope and be done with it than to love the people who leave their dirty dishes on the piano bench, which is not supposed to be a table anyway, and make you late because they just can't get out to the car on time, and sometimes don't lift the toilet seat when they go and you're the next one to use it. The family, I think, is God's cleverest way of getting us to learn the good lessons, making the classes small enough so that we *really learn*.

My children have become used to seeing strangers sitting on our couch when they walk in from school, and if it's a woman who looks a little stunned, and perhaps some children, they know we have another battered woman for a few days, here in a safe home while arrangements are made to get her away from a violent situation in her own home. There was Ellen, stains still on her dress where oranges had been thrown at her. There was the lovely black grandmother with the three children who had watched as their father had killed their mother. My impulse was to put my hands over my children's ears so they would never have to know that a man had killed his wife.

The world is a battlefield, and too often the home is a theater of war when it ought to be the safe, warm place we all can crawl into to be warmed and renewed. Family violence is in every edition of every newspaper. Is that the result or the cause of violence everywhere else?

————

Happily, I don't have to worry about violence in my home, just unpleasant disagreements. When two children come up against each other, I always send them to the garage or the bathroom to work out the solution between them and plan for better behavior. It works pretty well. Once when Katy was very small I saw her sitting up against the bathroom door, behind which sounded a mournful meow.

"What's happening?" I asked.

"Juliet's in the bathroom. Planning."

A major flaw in this program is what do we do with the *mother* when *she* is the one who is causing the problem? There are plenty of times, and my children will never let me hear the end of it when this gets into print, when the mother should have been sent to the garage. I can lead the children in singing, "Let there be peace on earth and let it begin with me," and within an hour I can blow it.

And incident I blush to recall occurred quite ironically during opening night of *Peace Child*, a musical play. I had read of auditions for it and felt it would be a wonderful project and would give the kids a feeling that we are not helpless, that we can do something toward world peace. Emily and Aaron had just finished being in a play, but John and Katy were interested and were accepted. The play tells the story of an American boy and a Russian girl who become friends and subsequently help their leaders become friends. Someone on the play committee who had one of my books of poetry invited me to start off the evening by reading a poem I had written about peace.

Just before we were to leave the house for the first performance, I presented John and Katy each with a bouquet of white daisies and a card congratulating them on being peace children and wishing them much peace and joy.

And then I blew it.

All participants were to wear soft, black, theater-type shoes. I had bought Katy some at K mart for $6.95, but for John's size thirteen foot the best I could do was Penney's for $17.95. I resisted spending that much money for shoes just for the play, but I didn't want John to feel like a makeshift peace child; I wanted him to feel like a first-class peace child, so I paid the $17.95.

I was just finishing putting on my mascara when John appeared at my bedroom door.

"Mom? Where did you put my shoes?"

Slowly I lowered the mascara brush, an ominous feeling beginning in the pit of my stomach. "Where did *I* put your shoes?"

"You brought them in from the car last night . . ."

Slowly I turned around to look at John.

". . . didn't you?"

I mouthed a "no" and shook my head.

"Oh," he said casually, "I guess they're still in the car. I'll get them."

"John." I kept my voice calm and low, exactly the way the children hate because they know how much emotion is going into keeping my voice calm and low. "The car is not here. Emily has taken the car for the evening. We are going with Kathleen in her van. The car is *not here!*"

"Well, where did Emily go? I'll call her."

My voice rose a little. "She and Suzy went to a movie. I do not know which movie. All evening long your black shoes will be in the back of the car somewhere and you will be at the play *without your shoes!*"

"Well, Mom, don't yell at me. It's not my fault. I didn't know Emily was going to take the car. And I thought you brought them in."

"Why would *I* bring them in?" My voice was getting louder and louder. Confucius had said that the greatest goal was to remain calm, calm under every circumstance. But had Confucius ever been a mother? "Once again John does not take care of his belongings! Once again we are left in a bind because John was not thinking! I can't take care of everything! The shoes were not my responsibility. John, you drive me wild!"

"Well, I'm sorry!" he yelled. And I yelled back. And we yelled for several minutes. In an hour I had to go on stage in my white dress under the spotlight and say, "Let us sing a lullaby to the heads of state. . . . Let us sing them to peace." And in an hour John had to go on stage with sixty beautiful young people and sing "All I want is love, all I want is peace." And here we were yelling at each other!

But I was enraged. So often, *so often* I didn't quite get things all put together properly. I was trying single-handedly to keep so many irons in the fire and balls in the air, or maybe balls in the fire and irons in the air, that I frequently dropped one or another. But I had taken care of my part on this. And now I had to go to opening night and be humiliated because my son would be the only one who didn't have the right shoes.

Kathleen's van honked outside and we hurried down the stairs. On the way out the door, I saw John's white daisies lying on the piano bench. "Well," I said, "I'm sorry no one cared enough about the daisies to put them in water."

"Oh, Mom!" John's voice was filled with hurt.

Had I said that? Had I actually said such a low, low thing? I wanted to bite my tongue, but the words were out and floating like brown petals.

We drove in silence to the theater, except for my trying to

make pleasant conversation with Kathleen. Appearances are important. Conversation. Costumes. Shoes.

At the theater it was determined that John could just wear black stockings. No one would notice. No big deal.

I stood in the wings waiting for the audience to quiet and the lights to go down and the stage manager to signal me to go on. I felt rotten. What a hypocrite! I couldn't go out and give a peace poem. A few feet away John stood, in white pants, white shirt, white tie, colorful sash around his waist, garland on his head symbolizing peace. I couldn't even tell that he was wearing black stockings and no shoes. There was my six-foot-one sixteen-year-old half man, half boy eagerly waiting his turn to go out and sing for peace.

I walked over and put my arms around him. "John," I said, as I drew his ear down to my lips, "I ruined the peace tonight and I apologize. I'm sorry I yelled at you, John."

"Thanks, Mom. Sorry I yelled at you."

"Break a leg, John. I love you."

"Love you too, Mom."

All right. I had been to the garage and planned for better behavior. I could go out now. The stage manager gave me a little nudge and I walked into the spotlight to recite my peace poem, having made my own peace.

7. The Day Our Ship Came in and Sank

I am embarrassed to write this chapter. *Really* embarrassed. However, I have just remembered that my friend Jeanie and her husband over in Gilroy, the garlic capital, lost a whole lot of money they had invested in rabbits in a deal put together by a good church member with a lot of charisma, who was going to make all the rabbit growers rich. Jeanie and her husband spent $25,000 for twenty-five rabbits and a lot of pens and equipment and feed and an assurance that there were long lines of rich people anxiously awaiting the skins for coats. This provided the whole family, of course, with enough motivation to get out to the sheds before breakfast and feed the rabbits and clean the cages and urge the copulation. The only one who got rich, however, was the man who set up the deal. My friend Jeanie and her husband only got mad, as well they should, being left with 250 rabbits and pens and feed, as the lines of rich people waiting for coats seemed to have thinned down a lot. (What do you *do* with 250 rabbits after the rich people don't want them?) Jeanie knew someone who had lost $100,000 on rabbits and another family that had lost their house, so she felt lucky.

And I also know that most families in this country have either tried or thought of trying some get-rich-quick scheme: multilevel marketing of hair-restorer products or vitamins, chain letters, slot machines in Las Vegas, the stock market, lottery tickets. And we all have heard of someone who has actually made a million in Amway.

———

Now that I feel not quite so embarrassed, I will tell my story.

Hank was going to make us rich. He was going to ensure our children brilliant futures with every opportunity . . . just as soon as he got out of prison. Yes, that should have been a clue, but we were innocent and optimistic and righteous and it was our turn for a break. And besides, Hank, during his prison term, had been converted to the Church.

It was years ago, before Gerald died, before we had all moved to California. Gerald had met Hank at the Utah State Penitentiary where he went on church assignment every Wednesday evening to teach spiritually uplifting lessons. One night as Gerald shook the snow off his boots at our back door, he looked at me and said with a laugh, "Blossom, have I got a story for you. There is a crazy inmate in my group at the prison, a fantastic, wonderful genius of a crazy man."

"Yeah? What's he in for?"

"He was framed."

"Sure."

I listened as Gerald told me about Hank Farr, a new inmate in the minimum security area, who had just been transferred from a prison in California, and who claimed to have been unjustly put away by the Con Edison people, who were after his vast geothermal holdings. The actual charge had been bad checks, and Hank claimed it was all engineered by his enemies to get him. Hank was a millionaire, on paper anyway, had made and lost many millions in his day, and as soon as he got out he was going to be back on the top where he belonged. I'd get to meet him in a couple of weeks when I went out to read some of my poetry at the prison Christmas party.

Emily, John, and Aaron, now seven through four, came with us, walking wide-eyed through the heavily guarded doors that kept out the outside world. A number of other children were there; volunteers had been encouraged to bring their families to the party. All day long John had been thrilling friends by insisting that he had been so bad he was going to prison. "Huh *uh*," they said in disbelief.

"Uh *huh*," he answered. "Cross my heart and hope to die, I'm going to prison."

On the way up I had said, "Now, John and Emily, you are *not* to go around asking the men what they did to get in there. That is not polite."

I gave my reading in the small minimum security chapel that had been decorated only with a sparse Christmas tree hung with little silver bulbs. I couldn't take my eyes off the man I knew was Hank, though Gerald hadn't pointed him out to me. Only one man of the maybe twenty-five who sat before me wearing their loose prison greens looked like he could have made and lost millions. He was as tall sitting down as some men are standing up, gaunt, face carved with deep lines, thinning brown hair slicked back, intense blue eyes staring at me from under thick, protective brows, a huge energy rocking his thin frame a half an inch forward and a half an inch backward in a rhythmic little dance like a caged animal preparing to spring the moment the metal doors clanged open in four months.

"That was fan-*tas*-tic!" Hank boomed as he pumped my hand when the meeting was over. "Fan-*tas*-tic!" His voice was a stream rolling over large, sharp rocks. It was as deep as the voice of God in *The Ten Commandments*, though perhaps not so divine. The heavy lines of his face formed a broad grin. "I've been waiting to meet you. You're everything Gerald said, and more. And those kids!" He looked over at our three children sticking close to the plates of cookies. "Angels! Listen, I cannot *tell* you what it's meant to me to have Gerald coming out here. Do you know what a fan-*tas*-tic man he is?"

"Of course."

Hank laughed out loud as if I had said something witty and slapped Gerald on the shoulder. "Ha-*ha!* Did Gerald tell you our plans?"

"No."

"Well, then, little lady, you better sit down." He took me by the elbow and led me to a folding chair beside the punch table and sat down beside me, offering me a cup of hot apple cider. Gerald joined us, basking in Hank's admiration of me.

"Hell, I miss liquor," Hank said, "but I guess I'll have to get used to missing it. I'm going to be a Mormon, you know."

"I heard. Congratulations."

"I think that's why God sent me here, why God let the Rat-Fink put me away, so I could find the truth. And find Gerald. Gerald helped me, and I'm going to help him. Wild Hank does not forget a friend. I tell you, I've got so many deals lined up as soon as I get out of here! And Gerald's going to be my partner. Give us a year, and you two are going to be so rich you won't know what hit you. And those sweet little angels over there—it'll all be for them!"

On the way home I grilled Gerald. "But what do you know about this man? Is he a fruitcake? Is he nuts? How do you know he's on the level? After all, he *is* in prison. That is not the highest recommendation for a business associate."

"You're right. Milt, the man who was leading the singing tonight, has been checking on him. Hank wants Milt to work with us too. Milt used to be with the FBI and so far everything Hank's told him has checked out."

"But no one could track down all those wild stories—that he was a top wheeler-dealer on Wall Street, that he was a courier for Pope Paul, that King Hussein wanted him to be his public relations man, that Nasser took out a contract on his life, that he's friends with Billy Graham. What if he's cuckoo . . . making all this up?"

Gerald smiled. "Then we'll have a good laugh about it someday, won't we?"

_____

Getting rich. I'd never spent much time worrying about it. Of course I fantasized that someday something I wrote might make it big and bring in fame and fortune, but that was just a daydream. In the meantime my books and films and filmstrips and articles were our major source of income. I hired Lynn Ann, a college student from Montana, who wore her long brown hair on top of her head in a twist, to come in three hours each morning and be with the children so I could go up to my room above the garage and work.

The day after Hank was released he showed up at our door in a white limousine with a telephone in it to take us out to dinner at the Hotel Utah's four-star restaurant. I, never having seen a telephone in a car before, much less in a white limousine, was pretty impressed.

"Real food!" Hank's voice cracked in delight as he spread the white linen napkin over his lap and started in on the rolls. Then he stopped himself and raised his water glass high. "To our Lord, Jesus Christ," he said loudly. I nodded my head and clinked glasses with Hank and stole an embarrassed glance at Gerald. Toasting the Lord was not an old Mormon custom.

Over dinner Hank outlined a few of the deals he already had cooking. He had been on the telephone night and day since he'd been out. "They're all still there. And they all still love me. Wild Hank has been missed!" Hank's specialty was to be a middleman between the big financiers and the large corporations. There was a multimillion-dollar hotel deal in the Bahamas. There was a deal to put private mailboxes in all the 7-Eleven stores. There was a major motion picture deal, for which Hank would insist that I be the writer.

"But Hank," I protested, "how do you know I can do it? You've only heard a few of my poems."

Hank put a large hand over mine and looked at me with hypnotic eyes. "Little lady, I am psychic. Don't question me. Ever. A few of your poems? You are one of the all-time greats. And that play you told me about? Next year, no question, it'll be on Broadway."

"But you haven't even *read* it."

"I don't *have* to read it. Hey, what is this negative energy? I cannot work with negative energy. You have to *believe*! That's how everything happens. *Believe*!"

While we were waiting for dessert, Hank excused himself, to go to the men's room, I thought. But instead he walked over to the orchestra leader, spoke to him, then put something in his hand. The orchestra leader smiled and turned to his musicians as Hank walked to the microphone.

"Omigosh, Gerald," I gasped. "Is he going to sing? Please tell me he's not going to sing."

He was going to sing. Lifting the mike from its stand, he listened to a few bars of introduction, bowed his head to get his

jaw as close to the floor as possible, and began. "Old . . . Man
. . . River . . . that Old . . . Man . . . River . . ."

"Oh, no," I whispered, my napkin up to my face. "Oh, no."
I looked around. Please, not here, not here in the *Hotel Utah!*
One by one the people at other tables looked up, puzzled, as if
they had found a beebee in their chowder. Then they looked at
the orchestra. *Who was that?*

"He jest keeps rollin' . . . he keeps on rollin' along." Hank was
in heaven. His voice was big enough and colorful enough and
sincere enough, but not quite enough on key.

"Gerald," I said softly, "I am going to die. Get me out of here.
The man is crazy. And if you have anything to do with him,
you're crazy too."

Gerald chuckled in embarrassment. "You're right, he's crazy.
But maybe he's crazy like a fox. Or crazy like Howard Hughes.
Maybe he can still *do* everything he *says* he's going to do. Let's
wait and see what happens in Las Vegas."

Gerald and Milt and Milt's niece Bonnie came back from Las
Vegas like hillbillies who had seen a skyscraper for the first time.

"Well, he's for real, Blossom. Hank is for real," Gerald said as
the three of them flopped onto the couch in our living room. "I
would never have believed it! The minute we walked off the plane
we were met by an entourage of men from New York, who had
been told that Hank was back. They fell all over each other just
trying to get to him."

"Really?" I was genuinely surprised. "I had decided he was
crazy."

All three of them laughed together. "He *is*, no doubt about it,"
said Milt, "but he's *real!*"

Bonnie, a slim, pretty blond of twenty, leaned forward and
spoke rapidly. "Carol Lynn, I talked to one of these men. 'Do you
know who you're *with*?' he asked me. 'I guess I don't,' I said.
'Who is he?' He told me that a few years ago Hank was one of *the*

financial geniuses of the country, that he had amassed huge fortunes and then lost them because he was too good to people."

When they heard their father, Emily and John ran into the room and threw themselves at Gerald. He hushed them and kept an arm around each as Bonnie continued her story.

"He said Hank's been a millionaire over and over."

Millionaire? Emily and John came to attention. They knew "millionaire." They batted the title around like "movie star" or "astronaut" or "king" or "queen" or "professional baseball player" or "magician."

"*Who's* a millionaire?" Emily whispered to her father.

"I'll tell you later," he whispered back.

"Anyway," Bonnie went on, "this man told me that in New York Hank would have three limousines waiting at three different exits of the hotel where he was staying because he didn't know just when he was going to have to leave to close a deal or which direction he'd be going in, and he didn't want to lose a minute because minutes meant fortunes."

"Tell her about Frank Sinatra," said Gerald.

Bonnie sank back on the couch and closed her eyes for a moment. "I will never forget that night as long as I live." Then she sprang back to the edge of her seat and spoke even faster, gesturing dramatically all the while. "Okay. Hank told us he knew Frank Sinatra, and that Sinatra was expecting us over at his show. We got there just as it was starting, and we were taken right to a table next to the stage. When Sinatra came out and started singing—you won't believe this—he saw Hank and he *stopped his number!*"

I gasped and laughed. "You're kidding!"

"He *stopped his number*, welcomed Hank, said how great it was to see him again, and *changed the words of his song* to make it a song to *Hank!*"

"Can you believe that, Blossom?" Gerald grinned. "This is our big chance," he added, dead serious, "for all of us. Hank's got the connections, he's got the genius, he's got the energy."

"Does he have the sanity?" I asked.

"*We'll* be his sanity. He has no family. *We'll* be his family. Whether or not Hank can make it to the top again may very well depend on *us*. And if he *does* make it to the top, we'll go up with him."

"Well, with all those people thrilled to have Hank back, why in the world does he want to stay in *Utah*?"

"He's sick of the rat race. He wants to be with real people. He likes us. He trusts us. He *needs* us. And don't forget, in a few months, as soon as Hank can stop drinking, he's going to be baptized."

We moved Hank into the apartment in our basement, and our lives turned upside down. Within weeks Hank had, on seven thousand dollars working capital invested by Milt, turned the downstairs kitchen into an office, hired a secretary, installed two WATTS lines, and established two corporations with engraved stationery to prove it: "Corporate Relations Limited" and "Funding Corporation of America."

"Doesn't that look a little *strange*?" I asked Gerald. " 'Funding Corporation of America' located at *Ninth East* in *Provo, Utah*?"

"Who cares?" Gerald laughed. "What's in a name?"

Lynn Ann thought we were crazy. She had been hired as a helper but had quickly become more friend than helper, and so felt free to express her opinion on everything from the children's manners to detergent brands to this strange operation in the basement.

"The man is nuts!" she said after I came down the stairs for lunch on Hank's third day with us. "Do you know what he has in the cupboards down there? Candy bars. Hundreds of Kit Kats, and he's passing them out to the kids by the handful. They think he's Santa Claus. I think he's nuts! And he's ordering me around like I'm his private servant. Have you seen the wallpaper he had me put up yesterday in his bedroom?"

"A little gaudy, isn't it?"

"Three walls of whorehouse gold and one wall of green landscape featuring the Parthenon! Do you know what he's got Gerald building for him now?"

"What?"

"A kidney-shaped table to fit across his king-size bed for his telephones and papers so he can do business and never have to get up. I don't think he's shaved since he got here. He's *never* off the telephone, says the middle of the night here people in Europe and the Middle East are ready to do business. Who's paying for all this? I just don't want to see you guys get screwed." Then she paused and added wistfully. "He asked me what I would do if I had a million dollars, and I said I would build a private school where kids could really learn, and he said that as soon as things come together he'll build it for me. Do you think . . . he could actually ever *do* that?"

————

One afternoon Hank, honking steadily, drove up in a brand new camper. The kids raced from *Sesame Street* to the driveway, shrieking, "Wow! Oh, wow! Hank, is this *yours*?"

He proudly stood beside the shiny blue camper with wood trim and held open the door. "Nope, not mine. It's *yours*!"

"*Ours*?" the kids shrieked louder and jumped up and down.

"Or it *will* be in a week or two, just as soon as one of our deals goes through. Right now it's just out on a test drive. Come on, come on, climb in, what are you waiting for?"

More reverently than the children had ever gone into a church, they climbed inside the camper. I followed.

"Ohhhhhh!"

"Look, velvet!"

"A sink! Cupboards! A carpet!"

"Television!"

This last was too much to bear and the children hugged each other and shrieked. Emily looked up at Hank in amazement. "Is it really *ours*?"

Hank scooped Emily in one great arm and picked up both boys in the other. He was more thrilled, more hugely delighted than that night in the restaurant when he had sung his heart out to "Old Man River." It was touching to watch him embrace my children. If every Wall Street banker, every president, every general would hug a child once a day the world would be better off, I knew that. This is what Hank needed, and suddenly I hoped more than ever that he would succeed, not for us or even for the children, but for *him*.

Hank groaned a little as he hugged the children tight and said, "Oh, God bless you." Then he boomed his great laugh and put them down, saying, "Soon. This will be yours soon. And this is just the beginning. You ain't seen *nothin'* yet! You kids are going to have it *all*. But now I've got to get this back to the dealer's or they'll come looking for me. Jump, jump."

The kids waved and smiled as Hank drove off, their future, their fortune moving up Ninth East, then left on Center Street and off into the sunset. As I watched I felt a rising discomfort. Was it . . . *moral* to get rich so fast, so easily? I had taught my children that hard work was the only way to get rich. But other people had sudden windfalls and got rich that way. Was it a sin? Did God want people to get rich? Sometimes (not always, but sometimes) if people were terribly righteous, God blessed them to get rich. This had all started because Gerald was doing good work out at the prison. There was some logic to it, some poetic justice. And, of course, if we got rich we had to use those riches well. We would, of course. I already had a long list of wonderful, charitable works I intended to do as a rich woman: feeding the poor, establishing agencies, dropping anonymous gifts into the garrets of starving poets, taking my brothers and sister on a family reunion to a Greek island, getting Gerald that great leather jacket he'd been eyeing. Well, charity begins at home.

And heaven knows, I deserved a break. I had been trying *so hard*, and this had been a hugely difficult year: my father had just died, Gerald and I were dealing with some major stresses between us, we'd lost a lot of money producing two record albums, and now I had just learned that I was pregnant with a fourth child. It was only fair, after all, that I would be given a divine break, or at least a break via Hank.

———

A month later Gerald was with Hank in the Bahamas, negotiating with Charles, one of Hank's old friends, who was a member of Parliament there. That meant *I* had to talk to the men from Los Angeles, who came to the house to collect the $15,000 Hank owed them for use of their private jet service. *I* had to talk to the telephone company, who wanted the $6,000 that had been run up on the WATTS lines, and to the company that had not been paid for the two IBM typewriters. *I* had to come up with $175 to pay the secretary in the kitchen down in the basement, who a hundred times a day answered the telephone, "Funding Corporation of America. No, Mr. Farr is not in right now. May I take a message?" (I couldn't let her suffer from all this; all she'd done was to answer the ad and expect to be paid for her work.)

"Look, Gerald," I said when he finally telephoned, "this is crazy. A hundred deals have been put together, but no money has showed up, not *one penny*. I'm through!"

"But it's happening, Blossom. It's finally happening. Charles is wiring twelve thousand dollars to our bank to cover everything. And he loves my idea for a Caribbean Culture Center like the Polynesian Culture Center in Hawaii. I'll be in complete charge of developing the entertainment. Tonight Hank's leaving for France to talk to his friend Dennis Edmunds-Hill, who's one of the richest men in Europe and is prepared to invest a hundred million dollars over here. Just hang on. How are you doing?"

"Gerald, I have got six dollars in my purse, thirty dollars in the bank, and no bills are paid for this month. My typewriter is broken. I'm writing by hand . . ."

"Just hang on. I think it's going to happen, Blossom. You've got to risk or you never get anywhere."

"I throw up every morning. I haven't been able to pay Lynn Ann for two weeks . . ."

"Listen, you thought I was crazy when I borrowed two thousand dollars to publish your first book, but where would we be if we hadn't done that? You've got to dream."

"The dryer is broken. The kids keep asking when their camper is coming . . ."

"You've got to dare, to reach for the brass ring when it comes by! Just hang on. I'll be home in three days."

Hank flew from the Bahamas to Paris, and Gerald flew home. We waited expectantly for word and tried very hard to dissipate all negative energy, thinking and praying on Hank's success, trying to comfort Milt, who was very nervous now that he might never see his seven thousand again, telling the Rolls-Royce people to hold up on the car Hank had ordered, and trying to placate the phone company. Lynn Ann has a vivid memory of those days: me trying desperately to maintain my sanity, in the kitchen with an apron over my swollen abdomen, making whole-wheat banana cream pies, and tap dancing to a little song I had written, "Everybody Ought to Have a Body."

Two weeks after Hank flew to Europe, there came a letter postmarked Los Angeles, and all of us, Gerald, Lynn Ann, the children and I, sat down in the front room to read it:

Dear Family,

I'm sorry to tell you that I am writing this from a jail in North Hollywood. They tell me I was drunk the other night and caused a scene somewhere. I'm sorry that I let you down after all you've done for me, but I promise to make it up to you. I thank God every day for you and pray his choicest blessings on you. I'm getting bailed out soon and I don't want you to worry about me. Things still look good with Charles, though he can't wire the money for a little while. Everything in Europe went fantastically. It's all coming together soon, and believe me, I will take care of you all when it does. Tell Lynn Ann I will take care of her too, and thank her for everything she did for me. Also Milt and Bonnie. Enclosed you will find a check for ten thousand dollars to cover you for a while. By the time this reaches you, the check will be good. Tell the children the camper is still on its way, and I want you to use some of this money to get them bicycles and some nice new clothes from their Uncle Hank. I'll call soon. Pray for me.

> With Love,
> Hank

The check, of course, bounced. We got a couple of calls from Hank, one asking Gerald to send him an important document from the box of his personal papers we had been saving and saying that a major deal was absolutely cemented and we would be hearing from him soon. We never heard from him again.

The telephones were taken out of the basement and a woman at the phone company arranged to have our telephone bill forgiven because in hearing the story she was convinced we had been taken and had done our best and also because she had my poetry books and loved them. We had a major garage sale to pay small debts. When our house sold, we paid off the credit cards that had purchased the plane tickets. The children gradually stopped asking about the camper.

Strangely, we weren't angry. Even I had become fond of Hank, protective of him. He was not evil. He was kind. And just a little too crazy. Maybe life at the top had spoiled him for the realities down at the bottom.

Finally, Hank became a legend in our home, an object lesson on how not to conduct your business affairs. And he became a fantasy too. What if . . . ? Every couple of years or so one of the children would say it. What if Hank came back? What if he made all his millions again and showed up, passing out thousand-dollar bills and Kit Kats and doing everything for us that he promised he would do?

In the meantime, in order for us to all to eat, we've kept working, me at my writing and speaking, the kids at paper routes and yardwork, housework and babysitting. But I did something wicked last summer. I didn't know it was going to be wicked; I thought it was merely going to be funny, but it turned out to be wicked, I will agree.

I was finally going through *everything* in the garage, throwing away whatever wasn't absolutely essential to our well-being, and organizing the rest. I took down a box labeled, "Hank's Things." Oh, my! Hank's things. I stripped off the tape, noting that mice had eaten their way through one corner of the box. It had been twelve years now since our adventure with Hank. Where was he now? In prison? Dead? Poor Hank. I shook off the mice droppings and threw away old court records and letters, then made a small pile of memorabilia for history: Hank's driver's license, a Father's Day card from a daughter I didn't know he had, a letter telling the Chill Can Corporation that a one-million-dollar check was on its way, a booklet on the Shroud of Turin, and a checkbook from Far West Bank in Provo, Utah, the checks printed for "Wild Hank" Farr.

Then I got the idea. Lynn Ann would love this. She would *love* it. It would make her day! We still saw each other often and every once in a while she and I reminisced about the Hank Farr days and talked about how we ought to make a movie script out of the story. I took the checkbook up to my room and giggled as I sat down and wrote out a check. Pay to the order of . . . and I wrote in good, outrageous cursive, "Lynn Ann Somppi . . . $5,000,000 . . . Five Million and no/100 dollars." Then I signed it with a flourish, "Hank Farr." Still giggling, I wrapped the check in a blank piece of paper and stuck it in an envelope.

I loved it. Lynn Ann would love it.

———

Two days later, just as we were about to sit down to supper, Lynn Ann walked in the door without knocking, as she always did.

"Well, hi," I said. "How's it going?"

She stood directly in front of me and only her eyes laughed as she said dramatically, "You will not believe what I got in the mail today!"

"Oh," I said with great interest. "What?"

She paused for effect, then lowered her voice. "A check from Hank Farr . . . for *five* . . . *million* . . . *dollars!*" She almost could not say it with a straight face.

"No!"

"It's true, it's true."

"Five . . . ?"

"Million dollars!"

John was the first of the children to arrive at the table. "What?" he said.

Aaron and Katy came behind him, grinning. They had been home the day I'd sent the check and I'd shown it to them; I was going to tell Emily and John, but I'd forgotten.

Lynn Ann looked at John. "I got a check in the mail today, John, from Hank Farr for five million dollars."

John laughed. "Oh, you did not!"

Lynn Ann raised her right arm to the square. "I got a check today for *five million dollars!* It's true."

John was quiet a moment, then said, "Mom, has our mail come yet today?"

I hooted. "Oh, you think *we're* going to get one?"

"Quick, Mom. Where's our mail?"

It took a few moments for it to register that John was serious. I was about to bring the joke to a halt when Emily walked into the room and John stood up in excitement. "Emily . . ." he could hardly get the words out. "Hank is back! Hank Farr! Just like he said he would be! And he sent Lynn Ann a check for five million dollars!"

"*Oh, John!*" Emily plopped down onto her chair. "Don't make me laugh! Five million dollars!"

"Take a look!" said Lynn Ann, holding up a check she took out of her purse. John reached for it, but Lynn Ann held it carefully, moving in a circle so all could see the five-million-dollar check from Hank Farr.

Aaron and Katy kept quiet. Emily looked as if that much money had been dropped on her head in nickels. There it was, printed with Hank's name on it. Five million dollars! John bounced up and down on his chair like a little kid. "That means . . . that means that *ours* will be coming too. He wouldn't send that to Lynn Ann and not one to us. Omigosh, I can't believe it! Oh, Mom!"

I opened my mouth to put things right. This had gone far enough. But it was Lynn Ann's joke, I'd let *her* stop it. No, it was *my* joke!

Transfixed, Emily walked over and put her arms around Lynn Ann. "Well, Lynn Ann!" Her voice sounded strange. "Congratulations! What are you going to *do* with all that money?"

I couldn't believe what I was seeing. This was not what I had had in mind. John and now Emily *believed!*

"Oh, I don't know," Lynn Ann said casually. "Get some new things for my day-care center."

"Lynn Ann!" shouted John. "You'll never have to work again! And when *our* check comes . . . !"

I couldn't stand it any longer. I ran upstairs and came down with the checkbook. "Emily, John," I said. "I'm sorry. If you want a check like Lynn Ann's—here. Write it out yourself, for any amount you want."

Emily took the checkbook and she and John studied it for most of a minute. Then Emily threw it on the floor and looked at me in horror. "*Oh, Mom! You* did this. How could you? Oh, I am so angry!"

Lynn Ann and Aaron and Katy howled with laughter. I did not. I felt rotten.

John groaned in disappointment. "You mean . . . ? Owwwwwwwww!"

"I'm sorry, you guys. I really am. I had no idea anybody would . . . I'm sorry."

———

Nobody at our house has mentioned Hank Farr since that day, but now and then I think of him and send a little prayer his way. Maybe he's in prison or dead. But what if . . . what if . . . ? After all, he used to keep three limousines waiting at the exits of his hotel. And Frank Sinatra *did* stop his show for Hank that night in Las Vegas.

8. One on the Seesaw

Being a single parent is a mixed metaphor. It's riding the seesaw all by yourself, taking some real hard bumps and running around a lot to hold down someone else's end as well as your own. But it's also sliding down the slippery slide by yourself, going as fast or as slow or as often as you want.

First, the slide part. Every time I start feeling terribly sorry for myself, something happens to remind me that there are worse things than being a single parent. Sometimes one of them is being a married parent. I have several friends whose major family stress comes not from dealing with the children but from dealing with the children's father. And even when the marriage is happy, just having a man does not make everything great. As a single parent, I have a few blessings to count.

I don't have to argue with anybody over how to raise the children. I decide and I do it. I don't have to settle for living in a little town, because my husband got a job there when I'd rather live in a big city. I don't have to schedule my getting up time and going to bed time around anybody else's. I don't have to see money go for a share in a private plane. I can maintain the housekeeping standard I'm comfortable with. I can come and go as I please. I don't have to deal with somebody else's neuroses or procrastination or maddening habits—that is, those that are different than mine.

I count my blessings when various married friends show up at the door, having run away from home, at the end of their rope. "I had to get away for a while," they say. "I was losing it. I just grabbed a few things and got in the car and drove." One had driven sixty miles, another seven hundred. I give them shelter and foot rubs and sympathy and philosophy and in a few days they go back home.

When you are single you have privacy and freedom. Lots of it. I know an older woman who finally married the man she'd been seeing for several years. After they had been together in her home for some months I asked, "So are you happy? Are you glad you did it?"

"Yes," she said, but then added hesitantly, "only sometimes I say to myself, 'Why doesn't he ever go home?' "

We count our blessings again when a friend in a second marriage says, "Really, if I'd known how hard it would be, I'd never, never have done it. My husband tries. He started out being very polite to the children, but now he growls at them and criticizes everything about them. I can understand that. If they weren't *my* children, I wouldn't like them much either."

But as we count our blessings, we don't get past the fingers of one hand. "Marriage may have its thorns," I read somewhere, "but celibacy has no roses." Finally it is not much fun being the only big person—in the bedroom, in the kitchen, at the dinner table, in the family room, in the yard, in the car.

Which brings us to the seesaw part, the bumps of being a single parent. So, you can make all the decisions yourself and not have to argue with anybody about them. Who wants to? You long to have someone to talk to about the kids who cares about them as much as you do, someone to help you decide if the boys are ready to take the road test for their driver's licenses, whether the second car should be a 1984 Toyota with 75,000 miles on it or a 1975 Maverick with 27,000 miles on it, whether to drive straight through from California to Salt Lake City or stop at Winnemucca on the way, whether to let Katy go on the school ski trip, what to do about the snails in the flower bed. You can talk to the children, you can talk to good friends, but mostly you talk to yourself. Being a single parent is like hitting a ball against a wall when you'd much rather have a game of tennis. Or having to play solitaire day after day and wishing for just one game of Chinese checkers. It's never being able to say, "I think I ought to discuss this with your father." It's knowing that you're solely, irrevocably, permanently in charge.

Sometimes being a single parent can be really embarrassing. Such as the time I delivered Aaron, poor fellow, for his first scout outing with a little suitcase instead of a backpack. (Well, *I* was never a scout, how was I to know?) Or the several times I took the kids to the park to bat around a baseball when even Katy could hit the ball better than I could. Katy? Her cat would have been better at it. It hurts always to have to write that no, a parent will not be able to drive on the scout trip to Wolfboro, and no, a parent will not be able to serve as assistant soccer coach. And you feel like a fool everytime you take the car in and look blankly at the man as he discusses fan belts and transmissions. (Of course, Nancy's husband goes into cardiac arrest if confronted with anything mechanical; I have to keep that in mind.)

A single parent knows that the next shift is never coming in. You don't even get out of the car when you bring Katy home from Brownies; you just tell her to tell Emily it's time for her dance class, and to remind the boys that as soon as they hear me honk to come out for their piano lesson. The yard, the laundry, the empty refrigerator—they're all up to you. No matter how tired you get, or how much you would rather be lying on a beach somewhere reading poetry, you have to keep going, going on empty, and trying not to let the kids see just *how* empty. (Of course, Bonnie has six children and her husband travels a lot and everything falls to her too. But at least she gets a phone call saying, "How's it going? Hey, hang in there. I'll be back on Wednesday." And at least she knows he's out there making the money that supports the family. Her job is tough and never-ending, but on top of it she doesn't have to do *his* job too. Once, before he left, he wrote "I love you" with luminous paint on the ceiling of their bedroom, and as soon as she turned out the light she saw it and stayed awake a long time looking at it and smiling. "I love you" goes a long way.)

As a single parent you're on overload all the time. And if you have, as I do, a tendency to be disoriented, you're sunk. Your mind is on twenty things instead of just ten. You get used to being called back to reality by a voice saying, "Mom, why are you waiting behind these cars? They're all parked." Or, "Mom, you know those eggs you put on to hard-boil? The pan is black and the eggs are all over the ceiling." Or, "Mom, don't you want to drive through the pickup place before we go home and get the groceries we just bought?" Sometimes you laugh, but if it's a day you're running on empty, you don't laugh.

Couples can feed each other energy, fill each other up. A single parent dips down into the solitary well until it is dry, dry, dry. But the children are still crying for more and what do you do? Sometimes you go to your room and lock the door and fall on the bed and cry. Sometimes you're too sharp with a child and then you feel rotten. Once, a woman admitted to me that she had grabbed her child by his shirt and thrown him against the wall. (*She* wasn't a single parent; we have no corner on frustration.) I couldn't imagine it at the time, but now I can. I feel guilty for the time I kicked Aaron and the time I slapped John, and I hope I never lose control that badly again, but you're not the person you want to be when you're alone and going on empty and you know the next shift is never coming in.

Ecclesiastes 4:10 says it well. "Two are better than one . . . for if they fall, the one will lift up his fellow; but woe to him that is alone when he falleth; for he hath not another to help him up."

Single parents have to find others to help them up. We have to become, in some ways, like families were before they became so nuclear, so bordered by the edges of their perfectly mowed lawns. But now that I think about it, *all* families have to do this, don't they? Even traditional families can't make it alone these days. I keep reading about the epidemic of alienation that young people are experiencing. So many no longer have a sense of belonging. They don't have the extended family, the intimate community, the solid group of people they know is theirs. *All* of us use, if we're smart, the larger family that, if we're lucky, we are a part of. I'm lucky. Some people's larger family is the neighborhood, the club, a group of one kind or another. Mine is the church.

When Brother Anderson, our home teacher and former bishop, asked me to step out onto the front porch after his monthly visit, I thought there might be a problem he wanted to discuss in private. Had Aaron been causing a disturbance in his Sunday school class?

"Sister Pearson," he said, "I'd like to ask your permission on something. We need a good service project, and the bishop has given his okay to an idea of mine. If it's all right with you, we'd like to paint your house."

Paint my house? I glanced over at the white wood, the off-white wood. The two-story house we had lived in for seven years now had gotten a little more off-white every year. And the brick-red shutters wre noticeably peeling now. Maybe someone who came once a month, a meter reader or a home teacher who came regularly as a representative of the Church, would notice deterioration more than someone who came and went every day—sort of the way time-lapse photography works. I just took it for granted like the very slow aging of my own face in the mirror. I never looked any different from the day before, and neither did my house. Besides, a major painting would cost a lot, and I had long since decided that I would rather give the kids music lessons than have the house painted.

"Really, Brother Anderson? Paint my house?"

"We would expect you to purchase the paint, but all the labor would be donated. It does the brethren good to get together and do things like this. Service is the heart of the gospel and sometimes we forget that. I'd like it very much if you would let us do this."

I hesitated. The ward had done so much for us a few months before, when the children's father had died. My Relief Society president and her husband and son had spent hours laboring in the yard. We had received food and flowers and hugs and cards. Sister Spencer, my visiting teacher, had made me put by my telephone a piece of paper and a pencil to write down all my needs during those final, dreadful days so that she could call every morning at nine and see that whatever the needs were, they would be filled. I was still thanking people. Should I accept another large effort?

"Well," I said, "if you really think . . ."

"Of course I do. We'll be in touch."

One Saturday and a half did it. It was like a barn raising that you might see in a western, or find in the pioneer past of my own people. Everyone seemed to get involved. The youth made a party out of tying back the shrubbery and scraping the window-sills. Brother Evans, a retired contractor who was brought over in his wheelchair to give a professional assessment and plan things, looked thrilled to be back in business. Twenty men at a time slapped shiny, white paint onto the grateful wood. Some of the men I had never seen except in suits and ties, and here they were in their old boots and paint-spattered Levi's, tromping around on my roof and climbing ladders and taping windows and sharing rollers and joking back and forth.

"Hey, Rob, do you know how many psychiatrists it takes to change a light globe?"

"How many?"

"One. But the light globe has to really want to change."

"Ha! Very good. Do you know how many Mormons it takes to change a light globe?"

"I heard ten different versions. What's yours?"

"Six. One to change the globe, two to give the opening and closing prayers, and three to serve the refreshments."

"How about one to write the report?"

"And to put away the chairs."

Brother Anderson watched the work with tremendous satisfaction. "You see? We're not doing this just for you. This is the most fun these men have had together in a long time. Just sitting up at the church talking about brotherhood doesn't make it happen." He smiled and gestured at the humming workforce. "This is what makes it happen."

Twenty men on one Saturday is not as good as one man on twenty Saturdays or fifty-two Saturdays or years of Saturdays. But it is next best, a wonderful next best.

———

At ten o'clock one night, I was standing in front of the furnace trying once again to make sense out of the instructions for igniting the pilot light. Usually, knowing myself well, I'd call the gas company and have them send someone out to do it, but it would take a week to get an appointment, and suddenly the temperature had plummeted. The kids were wearing two sweaters each and muttering, "It's *freezing* in here!" Even Aaron, the true handyman of the house, had given up on trying to light the monster and had gone to bed. The older kids had to get up by six in the morning to get to seminary, the early morning hour of religious instruction before school. Poor kids. At least they deserved the house to be warm while they groggily ate their cereal.

I opened the instructions again. What kind of a mother was I? Pioneers had an excuse to let their children suffer, but I didn't. There was no reason for fifty-degree temperature in this house. Where was my resourcefulness? I had a master's degree, didn't I? A person who had read every one of Eugene O'Neill's plays in one summer could certainly read a two-page pamphlet. But where *was* the "gas control knob?" Where was the "small burner compartment access door?"

My rage grew against the cold and mocking metal that hunched in front of me like an insolent android. I wanted to kick it. Suddenly I remembered my mother damning an uncooperative wringer washing machine out in Gusher and saying, with tears in her voice, "This washing machine is going to keep me out of the Celestial Kingdom!" Well, damn this furnace and its "small burner compartment access door!"

Maybe I could call Chris up the court. Our houses were built by the same developer and the furnaces were probably exactly alike. And maybe she was the one in the family who lit the pilot; her husband, the bishop, was away a lot on church work. But it was ten o'clock. I called.

"The pilot? Oh, I can't tell you a thing about that. Dave just lit ours yesterday. I wouldn't know a thing about pilot lights."

"Oh. Well, thanks. I'll call the gas company tomorrow."

"But it's freezing. Listen. Dave's still up at the church, but let me have him run on down when he gets home."

"Oh, no. He doesn't need one more thing to have to deal with. I'll think of something tomorrow." I tried to keep the martyr out of my voice.

"He'll want to do that. It should just take a few minutes. I'll send him down as soon as he comes home."

I turned on the gas log in the fireplace, bright enough to cheer a room but not to warm it much. Usually it cheered me, but not tonight. I didn't sign up for furnaces. That wasn't part of my contract. How did all this happen? Why did I have to be a *charity case* and make the bishop come down late at night to light the pilot light on Sister Pearson's furnace? I hated it.

About eleven-fifteen there was a light knock on the front door and I opened it to admit Bishop Sutton, still in the suit that served the lawyer and bishop both, smiling and holding a flashlight and a handful of tools. Just like a single parent's, a bishop's list goes on and on and he doesn't get a penny for it.

"Hi. Furnace man."

"Oh, Bishop, I am so embarrassed to have you come down here like this. As if you don't have enough to do."

"Glad to help. We should have this on in no time."

I'm sure it was not by virtue of being male, or having special spiritual powers, but rather from having done it year after year that allowed the bishop to so readily find the "small burner compartment access door" and to get the dang pilot lit so that, at last, warm air blew through the vent.

Having a man—even so giving a man as Bishop Sutton—come by at eleven-fifteen to light the pilot on the furnace is not as good as having a man stay through the night, every night, to warm the family as well as the house. But it helps.

And it helps to have Sister Hardy, who piles all five of us into her station wagon to drive to Utah because she is going anyway and she knows I hate to drive.

And Brother Moseley, who likes me in spite of the fact that I'm always making waves in his Sunday school class and who runs over with his exterminating equipment when I call to ask what I should do about the hornet's nest under the eaves of the house, accepting only a book in payment.

And Brother Jones, who takes a day off from work to drive Aaron to Camp Wolfboro a day late so that Aaron can be with us for the memorial service for his father and not have to miss scout camp.

And Brother Gold, who responds to a broken toilet problem, and Brother Porter, who comes over when the water heater floods the garage, and Brothers Christensen and Ririe, who help when they're called upon.

And Uncle David, who performs the baptism that a father ordinarily would, and Uncle Warren, who flies out from Utah so Emily won't have to drive alone to BYU, and Uncle Don, who spends long hours helping the children formulate their educational and professional goals and writing them letters and making phone calls to see how they're coming.

———

And Brother Hilton.

The first Sunday in May, Emily came home and handed me a blue and white handwritten invitation to the Young Women's Presentation. I read the date, looked at the calendar, and sank onto the couch.

"Oh, Emily! The twenty-eighth? I won't *be* here. I've got to be in Seattle that weekend, speaking."

"It doesn't matter. I'm not going to go."

"What do you mean? Of *course* you'll go. This is a big deal."

The Young Women's Presentation was the Debutante Ball for

Mormons. All the girls who were just graduating from high school—usually fifty or more—were presented at an elegant event.

"Yeah. Big deal," said Emily sadly, slumping down beside me. "All the girls are being presented by their fathers. You step onto the stage in the spotlight and they read something about you that your mother wrote, and then your father walks up the stairs and takes your arm and walks you to where you stand in line with him until it's over. Sister Wendel said if there wasn't a man I wanted to invite she would find someone to be my father for the evening. Do you know how that would make me feel? To have to *borrow* a father? Do you know how much I would miss my dad that night, how much I would wish he was still alive? I'll just tell them I can't go. Except . . . they want me to sing."

"Oh, Emily." What do you say at a time like this? I make my living playing with words, but there are no words to make it be all right, to even make it *sound* all right that Emily's father couldn't walk up the steps and take her hand and glow with pride and present her at the Young Women's Presentation. "I'll cancel my trip, Emily. *I'll* be there."

"No, Mom. The mothers will all just be in the audience. It's not worth your canceling your trip."

I pulled Emily over and laid her head in my lap and stroked her long hair. "Please go, Em. You need to be there. They need to have you there. Just think how bad they'd feel if you didn't come."

"Just think how bad *I'd* feel, Mom, standing there without my dad and everybody else with theirs." Emily squeezed her eyes shut and a tear trickled down her cheek. I had become used to Emily missing her dad, but Emily never got used to missing him.

"Think about it, Em. Don't decide right now."

The following week Emily decided to go, and the week after that she decided not to go. Then she asked Suzette's dad if he would take her, and he said he would love to, but he had to travel that weekend on business.

"Ask somebody else," I encouraged. "Who's another man at church you like a lot?"

"Well, there's Brother Hilton. I thought of him right off, along with Suzette's dad. He likes me a lot. Only he's going to present Ann, and that would make it awkward for her. I don't want to ruin her evening."

"Maybe it wouldn't. Why don't you talk to her about it?"

Ann was the first friend Emily had made when we moved here, and Emily had told me several times that she felt she and Ann were more like sisters than friends. Ann was a pretty girl with honey-colored hair, a wonderful violinist, a straight-A student who had just won a top-level scholarship to BYU, and Los Lomas High's recent homecoming queen. On Emily's last birthday I had arranged with Ann to wake her up to the strains of "Happy Birthday" played on the violin. I didn't have to wonder what Ann's response would be to Emily's request. There was never anything but kindness in her good brown eyes.

And in her father's too. John Hilton was a six-foot-four, slender man with graying hair and a wonderful voice that had an adolescent break whenever he got excited—and he was always excited. Brother Hilton was forever telling me how much he appreciated my writing and admired my children, especially Emily, whom he always called "magnificent."

Emily seemed a little surprised, but I was not a bit, when Ann said that sharing her father would be great and Brother Hilton said he "couldn't be more pleased, couldn't be more pleased."

I hated getting on the plane. Usually I hated getting on planes; I'd much rather stay home, but I was doing two jobs and speaking was an often satisfying part of what supported us. I could have canceled the talk, but I had never canceled a talk, and I would probably sell enough books this weekend to feed us for another month and pay for the dress I had bought for Emily's presentation, a simple but gorgeous rose, drop-waisted, V-necked number that made her look like a Greek goddess.

As soon as my talk was over and I was back in my room, I called home. "Em? How did it go?"

"Oh, good. Really good, Mom."

"You've been crying."

"How did you know? It was wonderful. The whole hall was decorated with flowers and streamers, just like a junior prom or something. I sang "The Greatest Love of All," and it went really well. And we took our turns walking out onto the stage. Ann went before me because she's an "H" and I'm a "P." Her dad came and got her and stood with her, and then, when it was my turn, I went out, and they read what you wrote about me . . . oh, thank you, Mom, that was *so cute*. And then Brother Hilton left Ann and came up for me and I took his arm and we walked down to the line. And, Mom, he stayed with me for the whole rest of the program. He didn't even go back and stand by Ann. And when all the girls had been presented, a man up on stage sang a song to us, something like "Love Is a Quiet Thing." And I started to cry because I missed my dad, but mostly because I was looking over there at Ann who was standing all alone and looking at me with her dad's arm around me, and she was crying too, and we both just stood there for the whole song and cried. Mom, Ann was *happy* to give me her dad."

––––––––––

Being a parent—especially a single parent—means you *can't* do it all alone. And if you're lucky, you don't have to.

9. Let Them Be There

Even believing in life after death doesn't make its approach okay. Or make it easy to watch three-year-old Katy stare numbly at her cat lying dead on the sunny pavement at her feet; or to explain to the children that we're picking the gladiolas to take to the cemetery, which is the place where the body of their grandmother is now in a casket underground; or to make it all right that Emily's second grade teacher, Miss Bills, died of a cerebral hemorrhage two weeks before she was to be married; or to sit down with the children and tell them that their father will not live to the next Christmas.

By the time you have to explain death to your children, you yourself are used to the idea, even though it still makes no sense, still sounds absurd. You've carried it around for years like a bad shoulder you have to live with because there is no remedy. You do your bumbling best to explain it, using the visual aid of a hand coming out of a glove to demonstrate the relationship of the spirit to the body. But you find there is something inside of you that still screams in protest. I must stop saying "you." There is something in *me* that still screams in protest. I am half New Testament comfort and half Dylan Thomas anger that must "rage, rage against the dying of the light."

It was soon after Emily was born that I began to think about death in earnest. Was it that I had come so near to the door that I could not avoid the knowledge that *coming* inescapably meant *going* too? I can remember, just a few months after first giving birth, awakening with a start to a huge feeling of betrayal. A thought was choking me: "One of these days *I will not be here!*" I stared at the dark wall in amazement. How could this be? How could I not be, at least not be here?

Three or four times a year I fall off the edge of sleep into that same horror: I, as I am now, am not permanent. I cannot hold the thought for long. Life floods over me, bathing me once again with illusions of immortality in the now. In the daytime I write faith-promoting poems about the meaningfulness of The Plan, and I believe them. But once in a while, three or four times a year, in the middle of the night, I have a premonition of the dying of the light and I rage.

There are four people I am responsible for guiding through life and toward death, and I am overwhelmed.

I think I took them to the rest home that first day for two reasons. I wanted them to see what the whole pattern of life was all about, what life looked like on its way out. We had no grandparents in the area, but so what? We could find someone. And, too, I believe we are here to bear one another's burdens, and I wanted the children to develop the habit of blessing and lifting others.

The children were agreeable if a little apprehensive. Emily's Sunday school class had visited a rest home and it had smelled terrible, and being around that many old people had made her feel like she was going to throw up.

"Well, let's try it once and see how it goes," I offered.

———

I called one of the local rest homes to see if there was someone who could use a visit. Of course there was. Plenty. Come take your pick.

We picked Lillian. She appeared less forbidding than many of the old people we saw that first day. Katy was two years old and looked down from my arms at the assortment of cavernous eyes in shrunken faces and bent, bent bodies with the same curious fear she looked at the strange small ones that rang our doorbell on Halloween. The boys, six and eight, took the scene in bravely; they had seen old people before, but never a whole garden full. Emily, now ten, found it the most difficult of all.

"I just can't touch her, Mom," she said in a desperate whisper as we stood by Lillian's bed. "Don't make me touch her. I'll talk to her. I'll sing to her. But I can't touch her."

"That's okay, Em," I said. "You don't have to."

Lillian's eyes were closed. Her skin was as white and thin as paper that might tear at a touch. I reached toward her and her milky blue eyes flew open, then looked around her bed as if she was seeing a vision.

"What beautiful, beautiful children," she said. "Who are you?"

Each of the children introduced themselves. Emily smiled and said her name, but gripped my arm even tighter and said under her breath, "I can't touch her, Mom."

"So that's who we are," I said as we finished our introductions. "And who are *you?*"

Then Lillian started to talk. She was starving to talk, and her stories fell over one another on their way out.

"My home is in Washington, D.C., you know. That's where I really live. I have a shop there. Four presidents of the United States came into my shop. I talked for ten minutes one day to John F. Kennedy. Such a lovely man. I had to close the shop when I had this stroke, but I'll get back to it. You'll see, I'll open my shop again." Lillian tried to raise her left arm that had lain quiet across her belly, but it moved no more than an inch. She burst into tears. "When I get over this stroke!" Then her tears were gone, like a little burst of rain that was over before you could even think what to do about it.

Lillian's face turned toward Emily and her good hand reached out as if to touch her. Emily took a step backward. "Such a beautiful girl," Lillian said. "What do you do? Do you play the piano?"

"Some," Emily said, "but mostly I sing, dance and sing."

"What?" Lillian tried to rise up to hear better.

"I sing," Emily said louder. "I dance and sing."

Lillian burst into tears again. "You sing? You sing? Oh, I was a singer! I sang in New York!"

"You did?" Emily was amazed. "You were on the stage?"

"Just in the chorus. But I had a lovely voice. They all told me I had a lovely voice. I was in *The Music Box*. Do you remember *The Music Box*?"

Emily shook her head.

"And I was in a show with Fanny Brice. You know Fanny Brice."

Emily shook her head again.

"Sure you do, Emily," I said. "Barbra Streisand played her in *Funny Girl*."

"Really?" As Emily's mouth fell open, I saw a reflection of my own surprise. This pathetic, immobile, fragile old woman lying on the bed used to *sing* on the *New York stage?* She used to be a *professional singer?*

Even as I felt my surprise I was ashamed of it. Why shouldn't she be? Inside the costumes of the little people on Halloween, inside the sheet of the ghost or under the witch's mask there was always a real person. And here was Lillian, dressed up in old age. Of course under the white hair and the paper-thin skin there was a real person. Forty years from now, if I were in a home like this, would a visitor stand amazed to learn that the little old lady who could not even turn over used to *be* somebody?

Lillian was a real person, and I'd better be careful how I used her. Used her? I wasn't using her, was I? I had brought the children here for an object lesson. I had selected Lillian as the object. I had trotted them in, all beautiful in their Sunday clothes, to teach them about old age and about being helpers. It wasn't that I had just acquired for the children a new toy or something, but clearly we were mostly here for *them*, not for *her*.

I asked Lillian about her family.

"Two children are dead now. My son back East calls me every Sunday, every Sunday without fail right around two o'clock. What day is it?"

"Sunday. He'll be calling in about an hour."

"And I have a daughter not too far away."

"Oh good. Then you see her often."

"No, she doesn't come. Only once in a long, long while." Lillian's face began to cloud up. "She can't bear to see me like this. She says she just can't bear it, so she doesn't come." Lillian cried for about ten seconds and then stopped.

I felt a wave of indignation. Lillian had a daughter in the area who would not come to visit because it was too hard to see her mother flat on her back with a stroke? I, a perfect stranger, was here, and her own daughter wouldn't come?

Suddenly I flashed on a fifteen-year-old girl coming up with every possible excuse not to visit her mother who was dying in the hospital. It was me. My mother had cancer and had spent months in the hospital, with a few brief respites at home. In those last months I visited less and less. It was just *too hard*! How could I bear to watch her get thinner and thinner? I was young. I wanted life, not death. I didn't want to have to go to the hospital and face the fact that my mother was dying. I wanted to be with my friends, who were alive and who would always be alive. I wanted to go downtown, where you *got* things not *gave up* things. I wanted to watch television, where people moved fast and spoke loud and the audience laughed and if anybody died you knew they were just acting anyway. Days would go by and I would find an excuse not to go to the hospital. More than a week, even.

After my mother's death, I cried about a lot of things. And one thing was that I had not gone to the hospital as I should have. I felt terribly guilty and held a picture of her in my mind, lying in her hospital bed, asking my father, "Where's Carol Lynn?"

"Oh, she had a lot of homework. She'll come tomorrow night."

I used to have dreams about it, terrible dreams. My mother was still alive and in the hospital, but we had all of us forgotten that she was there. Suddenly I discovered that she had been lying there for months and months, in the basement of the hospital, and I cried and went to her and tried to bring her home. Sometimes in the dream I managed to get her home and tell her how sorry I was that I had neglected her before she died.

In my adult years, whenever I saw an older woman in a hospital or in a rest home I would feel something stir in me and I would have to *do* something, take her hand, rub her shoulders, talk to her. And I knew I was really doing it to my mother, trying in some way to make up for having been selfish, for having been incapable, for having been fifteen.

"You sing, Emily?" Lillian was saying. "Will you sing for me now?"

"Sure. We'll all sing." Emily picked up Katy and pushed the boys in closer to the bed and led out with "You Are My Sunshine."

When they had finished, Lillian clapped her good hand against her thigh and her tears came again. "Wonderful!" she said. "Oh, wonderful! Nurse! Nurse!" Lillian continued calling until someone came, a tired but patient middle-aged woman, bent from turning people over.

"Toilet, Lillian?" she asked.

"Sing it again," Lillian demanded of the children. "Sing it for Beverly!"

The children started over and sang the song all the way through again.

"Great!" said the nurse, beaming. "Just great! Are these your grandchildren, Lillian? I didn't know you had family nearby."

"No," said Lillian, and she burst into tears again. "These are my . . . my friends!"

Beverly looked at me appreciatively. "Friends. How nice to have such nice friends."

I found myself looking at the floor. Why should I be embarrassed? Friends? Was I Lillian's friend? We had come on a field trip to learn about kindness and to learn about old age. We had come to find an audience and the audience had smiled and clapped, even if with only one good hand. I had come to make a belated visit to my mother, forgotten in the hospital.

But friends? Had we come to be friends? I took the word seriously. I knew that it meant caring, really caring.

"Kids," I said, "listen a minute. Lillian would like us to be her friends. What do you think?"

The children looked at me and nodded their heads. "Okay."

"A friend," I said, "is somebody who comes back."

They looked at each other, then at Lillian, then back at me. "Okay."

As we left her bedside a few minutes later, I leaned over and kissed her on the forehead. She smelled dusty. "We'll see you again, Lillian," I said.

"Will you?"

"Soon."

The boys dutifully followed my example and gave Lillian a kiss on the forehead. I held out Katy's hand for Lillian to squeeze and then took Emily by the elbow to leave. But Emily pushed in closer and slowly stretched out her hand toward the dead arm lying across the sheet.

"Good-bye, Lillian," she said, and gently stroked the near-transparent skin.

In the many visits that followed, there was something in it for everybody. We got a great deal of satisfaction from being Lillian's friends, and we added a lot of bright spots to her last seven years. We would try to think of things to tell her that might make her smile.

"Lillian," said Emily, "do you know what the boys said in the car coming over here?"

"What?"

"Aaron said, 'Mom, we don't have to go to school tomorrow. It's Veterinarian's Day.' "

Lillian chuckled. "He did? Veterinarian's day!"

"And then John said, 'Oh, Aaron, don't you know what a veterinarian is? It's a person who doesn't eat meat!' "

We all laughed again and Lillian told the story to everyone she saw for days.

Once we brought her and her roommate Geneva home for dinner. And once we brought them up to the church to see a musical play the children were in. (But after Lillian and I and her walker got stuck trying to negotiate the tiny restroom, I decided our visits were better confined to her territory.) And we sang her carols and brought her green and red Santa Claus cookies on Christmas Eve. And we read to her from the Bible and from Anne Morrow Lindbergh's *Gift from the Sea*. And Aaron brought in his guitar and amazed her. And we asked her over and over to tell about how things were when she was a little girl. And gradually even Katy noticed if we hadn't been there for a while and said, "Mom, isn't it about time we go out to visit Lillian?"

In January of last year, Lillian was not in her room. A nurse told us she had passed away a couple of weeks before.

"Good for her," said Emily, now seventeen. "She was all through enjoying life. Good for her."

―――――――

I hoped, as I went to bed that night, that Lillian went gently and did not rage much. And I hoped she had good memories to carry her out, maybe of my children, all dressed up, singing around her bed.

I don't like the thought of death any more than I ever did. If I were in charge and there had to be death, I would make it as predictable and as pleasant as birth. We would just curl up in a fetal position and get smaller and smaller until we were gone. (Nobody shuns a body on the way in, just on the way out; new babies smell so good and people fight to hold them.)

I'm on my way out already, and I hate it. I believe in God and heaven and life eternal. I believe we awake in some clearer place. But all I know for sure is one thing. We can help each other in the coming and the going. When our parts give out and our skin becomes paper-thin, we can gather around the bed and sing to each other.

Aaron has promised to get rich enough to buy me my own rest home and make it real ritzy. And John has promised to supply me with applesauce forever. If I'm lucky they can take turns keeping me in their own homes like my three cousins kept Aunt Mamie, and I can do their breakfast dishes and make the beds and crochet dozens of covers for coat hangers. I would like that. I will probably rage some. But Emily and John and Aaron and Katy will be there. They'll be much older than fifteen, and they'll have had years of experience with old people, and they will touch me and sing to me and make their children sing to me, even if they don't feel like it.

Please, God, let them be there.

10. How About a Nice, Cuddly Goldfish?

I hesitate to admit this, but I am not crazy about pets. I'm okay with human life, but I don't seem to have much knack for dealing with animal life or plant life. One can fake greenery around the house with silk plants these days. Not so with animals. Stuffed ones satisfy only so long, and while I do not need animals, I do need children, and children need animals, so there you are.

Don't ask me why I am not an animal lover. I do remember at about the age of three being treed by the family rooster and screaming from the lower branches for my father. And I remember at age ten pedaling fiercely on my bike to outdistance a bull that was chasing me along a dusty little road in Gusher (at least we were traveling fast in the same direction, he behind me). And I have a vivid memory of crashing my car into an elk that suddenly appeared on the highway; we both were stunned, but both survived.

Still, I have no reason not to like your basic domestic animals. The family dog, Gyp, was a comfort to all of us for years. But that's when I was a child and needed a dog. By the time I was a mother, especially the single mother of four children, what I needed was to simplify life, and the idea of a pet struck me as just one more responsibility, one more thing for *me* to have to worry about.

The children's first requests for a dog or a cat had been met with a counterproposal: "What about a nice, cuddly goldfish?"

Actually a goldfish was one of the first pets we acquired. John won it in third grade at the annual school carnival. I was willing. How much problem can a goldfish cause? Proudly John brought it home and dumped it out of the plastic bag into the goldfish bowl. It swam happily there on the kitchen counter for a couple of weeks.

"John," I said one morning at breakfast, "you have got to clean that bowl. *Things* are beginning to grow on the sides, and this is where we *eat*."

"I'll do it right after school, Mom," he said, grabbing his books. "I promise. Hey, could you just change the water so the fish will survive until then? Please?"

Fool that I was, I agreed. I have become less agreeable in recent years, but on that morning I agreed.

Never having owned a goldfish I had never changed the water for one. I took it over to the sink, fished the gleaming, squirming little creature out with a small sieve, and watched as it flipped itself out and slid . . . into the sink and down the drain! I stared at the drain incredulously. Oh, my word! I had lost John's goldfish! It was gone forever! How could I greet John after school and tell him I had lost his goldfish?

I hurried to the car and drove down to Steffi's, the local pet shop, walked in and said to the clerk, "Quick, show me to your goldfish. I have just dropped my son's goldfish down the kitchen sink, and I need to get another one before he comes home from school."

The young man looked at me disdainfully and said, "Lady, it won't work. A kid knows his own goldfish."

"Just show me to the goldfish," I said.

We walked back to the huge fish tank, alive with shining, darting golden flecks. I lowered my face a few inches from the water. All of the fish were exactly half the size of the one I had lost.

So I bought two.

I took them home and dumped them in the bowl and didn't say a word to anyone. John did not clean the bowl that night. John did not clean the bowl the next morning. But at breakfast he suddenly said, "There's two goldfish in that bowl!"

"Don't be dumb," said Aaron. "There's not two goldfish in that bowl."

John stood up and pointed. "Yes, there is! There's two goldfish! Look!"

All four children put their faces close to the bowl and then looked at each other in amazement. Then they looked at me.

"I cannot tell a lie, John," I said. "I did it. I dropped your goldfish. I dropped it and I broke it right in two."

Cats I have been a little more successful with—not necessarily fond of, but I haven't done any real harm to any of the several that have come our way, in spite of the fact that Juliet likes to use the artificial ashes in the gas fireplace as a catbox.

Juliet has been our main cat. When Emily was about nine and had been yearning for a kitty for at least a year, I gave in and took her out to the county animal shelter to get one. She had shown me pictures of the exact kind of kitty she wanted to get. It would be blond and cute. All of the children in our family were blond and cute, and of course the kitty would be too. But there were no blond, cute kitties at the animal shelter that day. Emily was heartbroken. When I saw her eyeing a skinny black and white kitty, I said, "Emily, we don't need to take a kitty home today, you know. Blond kitties are not the only true kitties, and there is nothing wrong with a black and white kitty, unless for some reason you would not love it as much, and then it would not be fair to the kitty to take it home. Don't be in a hurry. We can come back another day."

"But look at her, Mom. She wants me! And she *is* cute!" The kitty sneezed and Emily fell in love and promised she'd love the kitty no less than the one she'd had in mind, so we took her home and named her Juliet. She was loved.

A few years later, when Katy was nine, she was spending far more time with Juliet than Emily, who was spending far more time with clothes and makeup and telephones.

Juliet had already been sleeping on Katy's bed for two years, loved and tended exclusively by Katy, when one evening I was taken aback to hear her say wistfully, as she petted the purring cat in her arms, "Mom, do you know what? Juliet thinks that I'm her mistress. She doesn't know she really belongs to Emily."

All it took the next day was a quick word to Emily, who wrote out and presented to a delighted Katy a certificate of adoption, giving her full and absolute authority as the true mistress of Juliet.

My best memory of Juliet is the birth of her kittens. For a nonlover of animals, I think I did okay on this one. We knew that Juliet was about to give birth to her first litter, so I told five-year-old Katy to keep a good eye on her and to let me know if anything unusual happened. I was working in my office when Katy came running in, alarmed.

"Mom, Mom! There's a little blood on Johnny's bed and under Juliet's tail. Come quick!"

"Yay, Katy!" I said. "The kitties are knocking at the door."

Carefully I picked up Juliet and carried her down to her bed by the dryer in the utility room. I had washed her bedding the night before in preparation.

"Stay right here with her, Katy. Don't move."

Quickly I ran to the phone and dialed the school office. "This is Mrs. Pearson," I said. "I need to come get all three of my children right away on an extremely urgent family matter."

"Oh," responded the secretary. "Well, certainly."

"Can you have them out in front of the school in five minutes?"

"Of course!"

I felt a little guilty as I jumped in the car and drove quickly to the school. The school had asked us to try to make medical and dental appointments at times other than school hours, but they hadn't said anything about bringing children home to watch the birth of kittens. The secretary probably thought there had been a death in the family. Close.

"What's the matter?" asked Emily seriously, as the three piled into the car.

"It's a birthday party!" I said.

"What?"

"Juliet's kittens, they're almost here."

"Really?" asked John and Emily in unison.

"Put the pedal to the metal, Mom," urged Aaron.

When we walked in the house, Katy was in tears. "Juliet's run off, Mom. I don't know where she is."

After scouring every room and closet and checking under every bed, we located Juliet in the upstairs linen closet. All the children gathered around and peeked inside. Juliet was twisting a little and wailing.

"What do we do, Mom?" Aaron asked anxiously.

"Not much. Juliet will take care of everything. The only thing

I can think of is to say a little prayer for her. Emily, will you say it?"

We knelt down beside the open linen closet and closed our eyes and folded our arms. Emily prayed that Juliet would not hurt too bad and that she would have good kitties. No sooner had we all said "amen" than Juliet wailed loudly. We opened our eyes and watched in fascination. In a few minutes, something appeared, a little black, wet lump. Then another. And another.

"There's five!" Emily exclaimed after it was over. "But what's that other stuff?"

"It's the placenta," I said. "I told you about the placenta."

"But, she's . . . eating it! Oh, gross! Oh, sick! Juliet, how could you?"

We closed the closet door to let Juliet respond to her ancient promptings in private.

Unfortunately, none of the five kitties survived. A cat expert told us that Juliet was really too young to have kittens, but we didn't know any better and evidently neither did she.

"Juliet had a batch of kittens," I heard Katy explain to a friend. "Only they didn't turn out."

"Let this be a lesson to you," I told the children as we discussed it. "Teenage pregnancy is not a good idea. For anybody."

Emily rolled her eyes.

We decided that before having Juliet spayed we would give her one more chance at motherhood. The next year she had another batch of kittens. And they turned out.

———

And now about the boa constrictor.

I wasn't sure I heard right when John accosted me in the driveway, but then I feared I had. His best friend Mark was with him, a short, witty boy with wire-rimmed glasses, who shared all of John's interests. Both boys looked like something truly remarkable was in the works.

"Mom, I won a boa! Can I have it?"

"A boa? You mean one of those feather things?"

"A *real* boa! With a cage! They said I had to have your permission first. Can I? Please?"

"A boa . . . as in snake?"

"Yeah! Six and a half feet long!"

"Please be joking."

John's bedroom already housed a water dragon, a mud puppy, and some anoles, and he constantly talked and read about reptiles. He had long since concluded that the world would be far better off if man were eliminated and the animals were allowed to live in peace. I sometimes felt he identified with animals and plants more than with humans. On a visit to the doctor for a sore throat, the doctor had asked, "Have you been experiencing any other symptoms?"

"Well, yesterday," John said, "my dung was black."

"Excuse me? Your tongue was black?"

"No, my *dung*. My *dung* was black."

So I was used to strange things from John. But this!

"I won the raffle," he went on. "I bought three tickets at the Bay Area Amphibian and Reptile Society meeting I went to with Mark. The boa was the main prize and I won!"

The image of a cold, clammy, six-and-a-half-foot snake slithered into my mind. Unlike Eve, I was not tempted. But John was more than. John was electrified with excitement. I considered. Primeval antipathy fought for a moment with maternal devotion. Maternal devotion won.

"Sure," I said. "Why not?"

"Oh, boy!" John cheered. "Thanks, Mom. See, Mark? I told you she was a nice lady."

"Will he eat with us at the table?"

"He's a she," volunteered Mark. "And boa constrictors are not much trouble at all. She eats only once or twice a month."

"Lettuce? Spinach?"

"Rats."

Primeval antipathy raised her hand and opened her mouth to speak, but it was too late. John was on his way to the telephone to tell the man that yes, his nice mother would let him have the boa.

John's room became the showplace of the house. Wide-eyed neighbor kids traipsed in and out. Adult visitors said in disbelief, "Is there really a boa up there?" and then gallantly went to see or tactfully declined. After a while I got used to the idea and almost forgot there was a six-and-a-half-foot reptile just through my bedroom wall.

"Mom," John approached me one evening with a puzzled voice. "Have you seen the boa?"

I froze, then slowly turned to look at him. John broke into a great laugh. "Just kidding, Mom. Just keeping you on your toes."

Food for the boa was a problem. John determined about three weeks after she arrived that it was feeding time, and he collected his savings and went down to the pet store and bought two large rats.

"It's time to feed the boa," he announced after dinner. "Who wants to watch?"

"You are a sick and demented person, John," said Emily, who had not set foot in John's room since the creature came. "You are very sick."

"It's just the food chain," John replied. "I didn't make it up. Nature did. You eat cows and the boa eats rats."

"I want to watch," said Aaron.

"You would," said Emily.

"Me too," said Katy.

Emily groaned as she watched her three uncivilized younger siblings go up the stairs to watch the ritual.

A couple of hours later, they marched back down the stairs. John smiled triumphantly. "Well, she did it. Got 'em both."

"It was *so neat!*" said Katy. "Even the tails!"

Emily put a hand over her mouth and ran out of the room.

The last straw for Emily came when John brought home a bunny to be the next meal. The pet store had been out of rats and John had read that feeding a boa a small rabbit is the equivalent of two rats. So he brought home a bunny.

"Oh, how cute!" Katy said as she reached out to touch the brown and white fur. Then her eyes traveled up to John's face. "You're going to feed it to the boa?"

"Yep."

"Better not tell Emily."

Somebody told Emily, I'm not quite sure who. But after John had deposited the rabbit in the cage and left the house, Emily and her friend Suzy burst into my room.

"Is John feeding that bunny to the boa?" she demanded, with fire in her eye. "That darling little bunny?"

"I think he may have," I said.

Emily raced to John's bedroom door and flung it open. Her scream pierced the air. "No!"

The little bunny was huddled in a corner of the cage quivering. The snake was coiled up on the other side, just becoming aware that breakfast had been served.

"Quick, Suzy. I'll open the cage. You grab the bunny!"

"*Me* grab the bunny? *You* grab the bunny!"

"Okay. I'll grab the bunny."

With shrieks and squeals, Suzy opened the cage and Emily grabbed.

"Quick!"

"Help!"

"Fast!"

"Watch out!"

The cage door slammed and the girls emerged with the shivering bunny in Emily's hands.

"How could he? How could he? *Look* at that!"

"Well, now what, Em?" I asked.

"I'm taking this bunny to the Alexander Lindsay Junior Museum right now. They *protect* animals."

"But what about the boa? John just might go get another bunny. The pet store was out of rats."

"We'll find some rats," Emily said.

Two hours later the girls came back with a large, white box. "We went to four pet stores," said Emily. "It was *so gross!* I hate rats about as much as I hate snakes, and I had to hold the box on my lap all the way home. Every time we turned a corner I could feel their gross little feet running to the other side of the box. Yuk!"

From the hallway I listened to the girls in John's room.

"You open the cage and I'll dump the rats in."

Squeak. Bang. Shriek. Thump.

"Catch him!"

"*You* catch him!"

Shriek. Thump. Slam. Giggle. The girls darted out of John's room and slammed the door behind them, breathless and laughing hysterically.

When John came home Emily confronted him coldly. "John, somewhere in your room there is a boa and two rats. The bunny is being safely sheltered at the Alexander Lindsay Junior Museum."

John absorbed this information for a moment and then nodded his head wisely. "Emily, do you know what they feed the snakes at the Lindsay Museum?"

"What?"

"Rats. And rabbits."

———

Eventually John donated the boa to a veterinarian's office. The animals in the house now are not quite so exotic. Even a mother who is not much for animals can deal with it. Katy's hamster in its plastic running ball crashes into my ankles from time to time. The crickets John buys to feed the turtles sometimes escape and I wake at two A.M. with a cheerful chirping in my ear, grab a shoe, and chase a little black creature around the room, sleepy-eyed and cursing and never getting him. Jesse, the poor black dog that John found at the creek and decided was a gift of the gods to him, finds ever more creative ways of getting out and rummaging around in our and the neighbor's garbage, and has been known to eat all the newly decorated Christmas cookies and throw up all over John's bedroom. And Katy's puppy—adorable, impossible creature that she is—yips constantly.

But I can handle it. If mothers are going to be judged on their tolerance of as well as enthusiasm for their children's pets, I may squeak by. Just barely.

After all, every once in a while I say a kind word to Jesse as I let him out from the garage into the backyard. Sometimes I even pat him on the head.

"John loves you, Jessie," I say. "John loves you."

11. My Plaids Don't Match

Halfway through the talk I was giving I spotted a familiar face in
the audience, a round, smiling face framed with short, gray hair.
Oh, my word, I thought, it's Mrs. Jacobs, my old high school
home economics teacher! How many hundreds of years ago was
that?

I didn't miss a beat in my talk, but suddenly in my mind I was
back in the home ec room at high school in Provo, Utah,
listening to Mrs. Jacobs, along with twenty other young women
anxious to learn the skills that would be the foundation of the rest
of our lives: cooking and sewing. "Now girls, you *must* open the
seams and press them. Some of you are not doing that. Look.
This is a seam that is not opened and pressed. This is a seam that
is. Which is nicer? Well, of course. If you get in the right habit

now, you'll never have to *think* about pressing your seams the rest of your life, you'll just *do* it. And when you lay the pattern out on the material, especially if the material is a plaid like Linda's here or a stripe like Shauna's . . . hold it up, Shauna . . . up, up." We took our turns whirring away at the row of black shiny Singer sewing machines, trying intently to make our plaids match and our seams lie flat, as if it were a tenet of our religion. The skirt I finished was real cute, but the blouse poked out in places that I did not poke out in and so quickly found its way into the donation box.

I did better the next quarter in cooking. Except that my banana bread always, always had a crack down the middle. It still does. At least it did the last time I made banana bread. A year ago.

After my talk was finished, Mrs. Jacobs lined up to speak to me. "Do you know who I am?" she beamed, as she peered over her glasses and held out her arms.

I embraced her. "Well, of course I do, Mrs. Jacobs. Of course I do!" Still hugging her, I spoke into her ear. "Mrs. Jacobs, I have a terrible confession. I do not make all my children's clothes."

She laughed and pulled back to look at me. "Well, I'd certainly be ashamed of you if you did. What you're doing is much more important. Oh, I am *so* proud of you!" She squeezed my hands and I hugged her again.

Make all my children's clothes? I didn't even *wash* all my children's clothes. In fact, I didn't wash *any* of my children's clothes. For a couple of years now the kids had been responsible for sending their laundry through once a week and putting it away themselves. Why in the world should the mother do large batches of laundry every day and then sort it into five piles and fold and put it in closets and drawers? So what if now and then white underwear came out pink?

Pink underwear wasn't really what I had in mind years ago

when I was preparing for homemaking, but as the old saying goes, "There's many a slip 'twixt the cup and the lip," and one of the things that had spilled out all over the place was my idea of how family life was going to be. I was not, could not be even if I wanted to be, a traditional mother. I knew that even back then at seventeen when I was hunched over the Singer sewing machine. But now the whole notion of mother was being reconstructed and I and most women I knew were devising our own pattern, two patterns really, one marked "homemaker" and one marked "career," and laying them out on the available material and pinning and cutting and stitching as best we could. Usually, no matter how cleverly we laid out the pattern, there was not enough material, and we ended up piecing here and there, so that on both of the outfits our plaids didn't match.

My plaids don't match.

Some of us *have* to wear two outfits. Others of us want to. I do both. If I don't write, my kids go hungry; therefore I have to. If I don't write, *I* go hungry; therefore I want to.

———

My plane landed in San Francisco at about half past ten and I pulled into the driveway about midnight, pretty sure I would not find the kind of mess that had greeted me one night three years before. I had taken a rare day off to play in San Francisco with a friend, and when I came home I was met with the mess of the world. Dishes were on the piano bench and on the floor of the front room in front of the television. Shoes and socks and other assorted items littered the carpet and the couch and the stairs. Did I dare to enter the kitchen? Worse than I'd thought. Dishes, pans, silverware, leftover food filled the sink and covered the counters.

I stood staring as if it might be an illusion that would dissolve momentarily. How dare they let me come home to a mess like this? Well, I would not touch it, and in the morning. . . . *Forget* in the morning! I stomped to the fireplace and picked up the cowbell that you could keep by the bed to ring when you were sick. Well, I was sick, sick of these kids not taking their family responsibilities seriously, sick of being treated like a maid. I walked up the stairs ringing the cowbell as loudly as I could. "Time to get up, everybody," I shouted. "Time to get up and clean the kitchen!" I went into each bedroom, turned on the light, and rang the bell above each child's head until their shocked eyes flew open. "Get up! Get up! Into the kitchen, now!"

In a moment four dazed, barefoot children stood in the middle of the kitchen, red-eyed, hair askew, staring at their mother as if she'd gone mad. "*I will not have it!*" I said furiously. "Look at this place! A pigpen! Maybe you guys like to live in a pigpen, but I will not have it! And the front room . . . look! Come in here and look! Dishes! An apple core on the piano!" I lowered my voice to the level of serious threat. "*Who left an apple core on the piano?*"

No one spoke. Then Aaron in a weak voice began. "Mom, I'm sorry we forgot to clean up, but it's not a pigpen. It's not as bad as you think. Here's a clean place." He pointed to the rest of the piano where there were no apple cores, then to a large uncluttered place on the carpet. "And here's a clean place. There's *lots* of clean places!"

I was too angry to be impressed. "*I am going up to bed now,*" I said. "You may follow when everything, *everything* is in order." And I stomped up the stairs.

The next day I boxed up all the dishes in the kitchen and put them in the garage and then traveled from store to store until I found what I was looking for: a set of dishes of a different color for each child, plate, bowl and cup, red for Emily, beige for John, blue for Aaron, yellow for Katy. I would use the old brown and white ones.

"Maybe some mothers have time to pick up after their children, but I don't," I said as I laid out each set in front of each child. "From now on, except for Sunday and special occasions, these are your dishes, and *only* these. Each set goes in one of these plastic bins here in the cupboard, see? And each time you get a drink, you rinse out the cup and put it away. And in the morning if you have a bowl of cereal, you rinse the bowl out and put it away. There will be *no more* dirtying one hundred dishes and leaving them all in the sink. And if I find a yellow cup on the piano bench, you cannot convince me that little elves did it. I will know exactly who did it! I will know that *Katy* did it! And if the beige plate is not here for supper . . . John, are you listening? . . . John will have to find it and scrub it or go without. Are there any questions on this system?" The children looked at me cautiously and shook their heads. They had become used to their mother and her systems.

———

Now, home from another trip, I knew there would be a lot more clean places than dirty places in the house, especially as Lynn Ann was there for the weekend and would have made sure the kids kept things under control. I could just climb into bed and rest my ever-so-weary body.

But somebody was already in my bed.

"Hi, Mom."

"Emily?" I called, throwing my shoes into the closet. "Do you have a cold or are you crying?"

"I'm . . ." She couldn't finish.

"Just a sec, Em." I threw on my pajamas and hurried to the bed. "Move over."

Emily threw back the covers and I climbed into the little single bed whose tiny borders I hated. I had often regretted giving up the big king-size waterbed that had served my married days, but this room was also where I worked and I needed the space, plus the bed had sprung a leak that I couldn't find, plus I had been convinced that waterbeds were not good for the back, and besides who knew when or if I would ever again need a bed big enough for two.

I had not considered that I would still need a bed big enough for two. Very often Emily would appear at bedtime and say, "Mom, can we have an overnight tonight?" And I would say, "Sure, Em. Climb in." And she would leap into bed and the waves would make me seasick and she would laugh and we would warm each other up and then talk until we fell asleep. When I announced that I was getting a single bed, she looked wounded. I should never have done it.

"What's going on, Em?" I asked, putting my arms around her and kissing her shoulder.

"Life. I'm sick of it."

"Well, it's all we've got."

Emily turned over and buried her face in my neck. I knew she had been having a terrible time. She had recently returned from a semester at college and had just about cracked under the strain of having to be her own mother, coping with friends' emotional problems, still missing her father enormously, and suddenly belatedly having to deal with confusing feelings that sprang from the circumstances of his death—anger and rejection and wondering if maybe all that really did not have to happen at all.

"What are you thinking, Emily?" I asked.

"It's so unfair! Every time I start to feel happy I think, this isn't going to last, don't love anybody, don't count on anything, it's going to be taken away from you just like your dad was taken away from you." She burst into tears and her sobs shook the bed.

"Oh, Em, Em. I'm so sorry." I stroked her hair and kissed her forehead.

And then the telephone rang.

Who in the world? It rang again and I could tell it was the new line I had had put in when *Good-bye, I Love You* came out. Several people had advised me to get an unlisted phone number, but I didn't think it was fair to put out that kind of book and run, so instead I had had a second line put in, and both numbers were listed with the operator. In the eight months since the book appeared, I had taken hundreds of phone calls, some from people who just wanted to thank me for writing the book, others from people who needed to talk to someone, were *desperate* to talk to someone.

But I couldn't talk now. Not now. Emily needed me. Emily was more important than anyone. I would just let the phone ring. But I never just let telephones ring, and I had to press my hand against the pillow to stop it from reaching out.

Again and again the phone rang. Surely they would give up. But they didn't. Ring. Ring. Maybe it was an emergency. Anyone who would call me after midnight . . .

"Emily?"

"Go ahead. Answer it."

I reached over to the table and picked up the telephone receiver. "Hello?"

"Oh. Is this Mrs. Pearson?" A woman's soft voice was on the other end. "Is this the lady who wrote the book?"

"Yes."

"Oh. I'm so sorry to bother you." Her voice cracked. "But I have to talk to you . . . I have no one . . . and I have to talk to someone . . . and I thought that maybe you . . . I just found out that my husband . . . I'm sorry."

"No, no. I'm glad to talk to you."

Emily gave a little moan and turned toward the wall.

"Hang on just a moment, please." I put my hand over the receiver and spoke quietly. "Emily? It's a woman who really needs to talk to me. She's crying. What should I do?"

Emily's voice was flat. "Talk to her."

"But . . ."

Emily threw back the covers, climbed over me and ran crying from the room. I put the telephone to my ear. I'd tell the woman to call me back in the morning, or to call me back in an hour. I opened my mouth to say it, but I couldn't. I couldn't. Emily would be here later. I'd do what I could then.

We spoke for an hour and a half. I'd heard the same story again and again and again, but each woman who told it found it brand new and shocking and utterly unbearable. Her husband was gay. She had just found out and he had just left. How can she live without him? What can she tell the children? She still loves him. How could he deceive her? What's going to become of them? Can I recommend any counselors or do I know of any support groups for such women in the Boston area? Will she ever feel like she wants to live again?

When we hung up it was two A.M. I got up and put on my robe and slippers and went down the hall to Emily's room.

"Emily?" I knocked lightly on the locked door. "Emily?" She didn't answer. Of course she was asleep. Emily was never so angry that she wouldn't speak to me. I knocked again. "Em?" Well, we'd talk in the morning.

Waves of sadness and frustration washed over me as I tried to sleep. It was too hard. I was trying to do too much. I was trying to be too many things to too many people, and I couldn't. Emily would forgive me for not being here for her tonight. It was an emergency. But little emergencies kept happening all the time, little urgent things were constantly pulling at me, constantly distracting me, constantly diluting my energies and my attention. Telephones rang. Things that were even more important than telephones didn't ring, they just sat there and were ignored and put off and taken for granted. The things that mattered most were often at the mercy of the things that mattered least. There was a long list of things I was going to do for or with each child when I had the time. But a ring never pierced the air saying this is the time, and only some of the important things I wanted to do had been done. Lots of times someone should have grabbed the cowbell and rung it in my ears to remind me of the things I had neglected.

I was going to start a monthly family newspaper with John as editor, and he was excited about the idea, but I didn't have time. I was going to organize all the good recipes we liked and have each child develop a file of their own, but I didn't have time. I was going to make for them a tape recording of me singing the Hebrew songs I learned on the kibbutz, but I didn't have time. I was going to read to the kids all the histories of their ancestors, but I didn't have time. And then *they* didn't have time.

I knew the words: "No other success can compensate for failure in the home." Our home was not a failure, but in the middle of the night, when I knew Emily had cried herself to sleep without me, I was inundated with visions of all the times I had done it wrong.

What would my children remember of me as a working mother? The times when I was sharp with them when they had interrupted my writing for the fourth time on a summer afternoon, wanting to be driven to the swimming pool because it was too hot to even ride a bike? "Would you call me at work if I were a teacher or a doctor and ask me to drop everything and run you somewhere?" I would ask accusingly. "I've got to get this in the mail or we will all be in big trouble."

Come to think about it, while my children were proud of my writing, they sometimes did not see it as real work. Once Katy stood beside my desk, watching my aerobic typing, and said, "Mom, all my friends' mothers work. How come you don't get a job?"

Working at home had its advantages and its disadvantages: the commute was only fourteen stairs and a hall, I didn't have to drop the kids off at a babysitter, I was always here when they came home, sort of here, kind of available, performing my ultimate Libra balancing act, walking around with hands out like the scales, "homemaker" on one hand, "working mother" on the other hand, trying to pick myself back up when I fell to one side or the other, which I always did.

Would they remember the times I couldn't go to open house at school because I was traveling? ("Are you kidding?" said John when asked. "Big deal.") The times when I had left my work but still couldn't really address the problem of the boil on the dog's back because I was preoccupied with the fact that I had to have all the tax stuff ready for tomorrow and I didn't? Would Katy remember that sometimes when we played Trivial Pursuit I had my checkbook open and would pay a bill while it was her turn? Would John remember the time I served the big batch of turkey soup three times in one week and he looked down at his bowl and said, "Déjà vu!" Would Aaron remember saying to me just before the approach of Christmas, "Mom, I *hate* holidays around here. You get *so stressed out!*"

Being a working mother was tough. Sometimes it was a mess.

But there were the clean places. That's what we had to do, keep our eye on the clean places Aaron had pointed out. "Look, there's a clean place," we had to say to ourselves. "And over there, there's a clean place!" Of course there were a lot of clean places in my own mess, ways in which the children had benefited from having a working mother.

There was the summer I wrote the pioneer Indian novel and read a chapter every other day to the kids after supper, and when I finished one night John said, "That's all? What happens next?" "Well, I don't know, John. It's not written yet." "Mom," he said, pointing, "get to that typewriter fast!"

My kids have had the fun of seeing me on television, of traveling with me on speaking engagements, and of learning about the various subjects that have found their way into my writing.

And they have had to become—as have most of the children of the working mothers I talk to—pretty independent. John makes better spaghetti than I do, Katy makes better cornbread, Aaron mops faster than I do, and Emily puts away groceries more efficiently than I ever will.

A friend who's a nurse who has to be at work at six-thirty tells me her sister is amazed the kids can get out the door every morning on their own. "Mine could never make it without my feeding them and walking them to the door and handing them their stuff," she said. (But here I must acknowledge that plenty of kids with nonworking mothers also become independent; still, I think they have to resist the temptation of being too well cared for.)

My friend Susan, who has worked in construction and interior design for years, remembers her nine-year-old Sara with a caulking gun in her hand, squirting the stuff around the windows. Sara is now preparing for a career in architectural design.

And my friend Pat, who has been city editor of the local newspaper, tells me her children loved it, especially the time she happened to cover a major robbery and her story and pictures were bought by *The New York Times*. They looked at her with new eyes.

————

Those are a few of the clean places. We've all got them. I don't regret for a moment trying to wear two outfits, hard though it's been. The experiences the family has had together might finally be more nourishing than if the kids had come home to a plate of fresh cookies every day. And they will always know that a mother is a real person too, not just a household appliance, and that she has a right to a life of her own, whether she wants to or whether she has to and whether her plaids match or not.

12. "And What Do We Learn from *This*?"

I was a little taken aback a couple of weeks before Halloween when I asked five-year-old Katy what she wanted to go as and she replied, "A mother." A mother. Really? Something *that frightening*? Here they come, folks. A monster, a witch, a mother.

I am not scary, really, just a little too grim sometimes. I am the kind of mother who tries too hard. But it seems to take more effort than I can muster *not* to try too hard, so I just go on trying too hard. Overkill, that's my kind of mothering. I teach my children as if I am the final gas station between here and Reno and they'll get stuck in the desert if I don't pump them full right up to the top. I teach my children as if they cannot read regular print and so I have to put it on a poster all in caps and underlined and then wave it at them. I teach my children as if, without me, they will return to the jungle. Fortunately, my children have a sense of humor even when I don't. Usually I have a sense of humor. But not when it comes to *TEACHING MY CHILDREN*. (That is to be read, as it is *done*, with teeth together.)

Obviously, when a child is three or four and breaks a window because he was throwing the ball too close to the house, cause and effect have to be pointed out. You pick up the pieces so nobody gets a cut foot and you sit down on the curb and comfort Aaron and forgive him and wisely say, "Well, Aaron, what do we learn from *that*?"

And Aaron, grateful for such a comforting, forgiving, wise mother, says between sniffs, wiping his nose on his shirt sleeve, "We learn . . . that we don't . . . throw the ball so . . . close to the house."

"Right, Aaron!" And you feel like a successful mother and inside you are saying, "He got it! He got it!"

And when Katy at age seven splits her chin open riding too fast down the court on Aaron's skateboard, you take her in for stitches and give her some aspirin and put her to bed. And as you kiss her and tuck the pink Holly Hobbie quilt around her, you say, "Well, Katy, what do we learn from *that*?"

Katy, exhausted and shaken, touches the bandage on her chin and looks at her good mother gratefully and says, "We learn . . . that we don't ride the skateboard too fast down the court."

"Right!" The mother smiles, knowing that tomorrow we will not have to make another trip with Katy to the emergency room for stitches, which we surely would have had to do if the mother had not written it out on a poster and waved it until Katy "got it!"

The children's lives with their mother have been fraught with learning.

"We learn that cats do not *like* to be put in the dryer."

"We learn that we put our dark clothes in *one* batch and our white clothes in *another* batch."

"We learn that if we don't put in *all* the ingredients, the cookies taste real funny."

"We learn that our teacher does not like to be called by his first name."

"We learn that the toilets in the bathroom display at Sears are not there to be used."

"We learn that if we start shoplifting, we too could end up in the penitentiary."

———

Now some of that is necessary. But how did I take it so far? How did I get to the point of *always pointing it out*? Of taking all the values I so want my children to learn and force-feeding them? The first rule I learned about writing was, "Don't tell them, *show them*." No one told me that was also the first rule of mothering. It's like Harry Emerson Fosdick said about vital religion being like good music: "It needs no defense, only rendition. A wrangling controversy in support of religion is as if the members of the orchestra should beat the folks over the head with their violins to prove that the music is beautiful."

I do that. I beat my children over the head with values to prove that the values are good. And it's a shame that it's only dawning on me now, when one child is already gone and two others are poised for flight. Isn't there something wrong with a system in which, when you're finally competent, you're obsolete? But, as I say, the children have fine senses of humor. As far as I can tell, they're not damaged. It's just that the mother is a little overweary from trying so hard!

———

When I try hard (that's *hard* with teeth together), the children laugh. And when the children laugh and I am trying *hard*, I cry.

The first such occasion that leaps to my memory is a time when the older children were ten, eight, and seven and sitting on the couch waiting to be *taught,* and Katy was in bed, unaware of how lucky she was. I had checked out from the library a book of Aesop's fables and was diligently going through them with the children, very pleased with myself for being such a good mother. This night I had even lighted the gas log in the family room to make a comfortable, pleasant environment for our learning experience.

"How long is this going to take, Mom?" asked Aaron, tossing a marble from hand to hand.

"Just a little while," I replied, confiscating the marble.

"That's what you *always* say, and then it takes ninety-five hours."

"It'll take a lot longer if you keep talking, my dear. Who wants to read this one?"

"I will." Emily tossed her ponytail self-righteously and reached for the book. "The boys are being too bratty tonight. As usual."

"Oh, huh!" grunted Aaron and took off one of his tennis shoes and began pulling the broken lace from hole to hole.

"The Sun and the Wind," began Emily.

Suddenly Aaron shoved his dirty-stockinged foot into John's face and laughed riotously as John recoiled with a "Yuk!"

"Aaron!" I chastised sharply. "Do you want to sit on a bar stool? One more . . ."

"No." Aaron could hardly speak for laughing.

John grabbed Aaron's foot and clamped his teeth onto the toes as Aaron yelped and laughed louder.

"John! Sit up, both of you. Sit up! This is not the playground. You'll both be on bar stools if you can't sit together on the couch. Is that what you want, to sit on the bar stools?"

"No," the boys managed to say through their giggles.

"Now, settle down. We're not going on until you've settled

down. Aaron? Don't look at John. I said don't even *look* at him. There. Are you ready?"

They were quiet for a moment, Aaron staring at the rug. Then he stole a quick glance at his brother and both of them broke into a stifled laugh.

"I'm sorry, Mom," said John. "I can't help it."

"Of course you can help it. And you'd *better* help it. Now are you ready?"

Aaron, hand over his mouth and eyes shut to keep anything from leaking out, nodded his head like a mischievous elf. John pressed his hands down his cheeks to get rid of a smile, making little curved windowsills of his lower eyelids. "Ready."

Emily gathered her legs under her, yoga fashion, and spoke slowly and condescendingly, her lips enjoying the words. "I will begin again: ' "The Sun and the Wind." One day the sun and the wind were having an argument. The sun said, "I am the stronger," and the wind said, "No, I am the stronger." So they decided to have a contest and . . .' "

Emily finished reading the fable and I turned to John. "John, can you tell us why kindness works better than force? What did the sun learn from the wind?"

John thought for a minute and couldn't resist. "Not to cry wolf," he said soberly.

At that Aaron gleefully punched John's shoulder and both boys burst again into laughter. Without a word I strode to the counter and pulled out two of the bar stools and arranged them three feet apart in front of the couch. "John?" I pointed to one stool, then to the other. "Aaron?"

"Why me?" responded Aaron indignantly. "I didn't say it. John did!"

My reply was another gesture at the bar stools and a fierce, fierce stare at my sons.

"Come on, Aaron," John said, climbing up onto the round oak

stool. "Sorry, Mom." In a moment, Aaron, grumbling, slowly moved to the other stool.

I breathed deeply for a few moments, the way I was taught to do in speech classes, and then I took the book from Emily. I would not let the boys win. I *would* control them. I *would* inspire them. They would hear the story of the sun and the wind and listen to my meaningful discussion and *they would enjoy it!* The fire continued to try to make the room pleasant, but it was a losing battle. "I want one of you to tell me . . . one of the *boys* to tell me," I said with my teeth together, "why kindness works better than force. This is an important story. We need to understand this story, lots of stories, so that we don't make all the mistakes ourselves. If we learn from others, we can prevent . . ." As I searched for the right word, Aaron found it.

"Forest fires," he squealed. Both he and John hooted so wildly that they nearly fell off the bar stools, and Aaron threw his laceless tennis shoe into the air.

I stood up and threw the book on the floor. "I have had enough," I shouted. "Get into the bathroom and don't come out until I call you. I cannot *believe* such rudeness!"

Still giggling and with halfhearted apologies, the boys made their way to the bathroom and I slammed the door after them, then stomped back into the family room. The fire had stopped trying. "Are those boys ever going to grow up?" I said on the verge of tears. "Ever? Ever?"

"Grow up? Mom, John and Aaron are totally disgusting, but they *are* only seven and eight. They'll probably grow up sometime."

"If I live long enough."

Yells came from the bathroom. "Mom! Mom! Johnny's throwing water on me!" Then some thumps. And laughs. And more yells. "Mom! Aaron's killing me! Help!"

I flung open the bathroom door, outrage beating its way up

from my abdomen. By the time it got to my arms and hands I grabbed each boy by an ear. "Piercing the ears" as my children called it was the closest I ever got to child abuse. I could skillfully press a fingernail into an ear lobe to obtain a one-hundred-and-twenty-volt shock that settled people down right away.

"Ouch, Mom! Owwwww!"

By the time the outrage got to my eyes, I could feel it squeezing out in little wet drops. I could feel my face dissolving. *"How dare you . . ."* I began. The boys stared at me wide-eyed and I let go of their ears. So this was it, was it? They wouldn't see the seriousness of the situation until their mother burst into tears right in front of them. Good. They deserved to see me cry. Now they would pay attention. The boys continued to stare at me for another couple of seconds, and then, as if on cue, they burst into an astonished laugh. Their eyes were fastened firmly on my contorted face as they laughed hysterically.

"Get into bed," I screamed. "Into bed right now!" Sobbing, I ran out of the bathroom and to the front door, grabbing my coat on the way.

"Where are you going, Mom?" asked Emily, alarm in her voice.

"For a walk!"

"It's raining!"

"I don't care!" I slammed the front door, hoping it could be heard in every room of the house.

I walked and cried for an hour or more. I knew it wasn't just the boys. Sometimes they *were* thoughtless and rude and they shouldn't be allowed to get away with it. But it wasn't just them. It was me; it was the whole, lousy, unfair business of having to do this all alone. It was caring so much, wanting to teach them so much, trying *so hard* and having it be uphill all the way. Alone and uphill.

Of course I finally went home. Of course the mother doesn't

walk in the rain forever. The mother goes home. The mother tries again.

"They're in bed," said Emily, as I came in, taking off my wet shoes and wet coat and grabbing a towel for my hair. "I made them stay. Boy, you're wet. I'm sorry, Mom."

I went into Aaron's room first. He had picked up all the clothes from the floor and tidied everything up, something that always accompanied a repentance.

"Sorry, Mom," he said gruffly from the bed.

"Aaron," I said as I sat down beside him and touched his arm, "you have got to understand how hard it is to be a mother, especially to be the only big person in the house. It's the hardest thing I've ever tried to do in my whole life. Ever. Much harder than trying to write a book or anything else. When I'm trying to do something important and I get no cooperation, I feel like giving up. Can you understand that?"

"Yeah. Sorry, Mom."

I entered John's room prepared to give the same little lecture. But instead, John sat up in his bed and began to lecture me. "Mom," he said firmly, "you are thirty-nine years old and you've had thirty-nine years of practice on how to control your laughter. But I'm just a little kid. I'm just eight years old and I can't do that. And when I see a face that I've never seen before it makes me have to laugh."

"A face you've never seen before? You've never seen me cry in your whole life?"

"No! Not until today! I know it wasn't funny to you, but your face was about the funniest thing I'd ever seen! And I'm just a little kid and before I knew it I had to laugh! You can't expect me to be as developed as you are. And another thing, Mom." John sat up straighter to continue his lecture. "You said that kindness works better than force, and it certainly wasn't very kind to pierce our ears like that. And besides, I already learned about kindness, like when we take in those battered women and stuff like that."

———

I'm a slow learner. I don't pierce the children's ears anymore and they haven't reduced me to tears for quite some time. But I still try too hard. Seems like I *have* to try too hard. But I'm becoming more aware of it.

A few months ago, as we were driving home from a movie, Aaron said to me, "Mom, do you know how much I *hate* to go to movies with you? I just *hate* it. We can't just see a movie. Oh, no. We have to talk about the movie and what the movie means and what we learn from the movie."

"Yeah," John agreed. "You're a nice lady and everything, and I appreciate everything you're trying to do, but, Mom, you talk too much."

———

Well, what do I learn from *that*?

13. "But if You're *Really* in Love ... !"

The easy time is before they're twelve and don't take showers without being told and make the throw-up sound if you ask if they have a crush on someone. Like Katy. Last year when she was twelve and I was sitting on her bed with her, discussing whether or not her room met local sanitation standards, I saw that she had written a list of names on the side of her dresser and drawn a large heart around it.

"Well, what's this?" I asked. "Are those the names of the boys you like?"

She turned to me with her most disgusted look and said, "No, Mom. Those are the names of *horses* I like!"

That is the easy time. A child being in love with horses does not make a parent lie awake at night. I get worried, however, when the kids start using deodorant of their own free will. I know they're responding to a call that will inevitably take them into the most troubled of waters. I guess there are none of life's waters that a parent worries more about. What can provide more disasters, pain, scars, and just plain heartache then the inevitable dealings with love and sex?

It seemed so easy when I was growing up, and where I was growing up. The voices on the radio in Utah Valley filled our minds with, "How Much Is that Doggie in the Window?" and "You'll Never Walk Alone." Today my little girl sits by me in the car and sings, "Let's Get Physical."

In my adolescence I watched *I Love Lucy* and *The George Burns and Gracie Allen Show* and *Hit Parade*, with its clean smiles and full skirts and pure romance. My children turn on MTV and are mesmerized by frozen faces and purple hair and violent movements and words that (when you can understand them) are harsh and sexual and women who are only bodies, and a camera that seems to have the personality of a rapist.

When I was ten my brother showed me a little flip book he had traded a jackknife for. You flipped the pages with your thumb to see a fan dancer go through a routine that exposed her cartoon breasts and buttocks. A few years ago Katy and I picked up some magazine pages littering the lawn at the park. They turned out to be pornographic photographs that quickly etched themselves on our unwelcoming minds. And when Aaron was ten and he and I went to a used record store so he could buy a present for John's birthday, we turned around from the Beatles section to see *Virgin Killers*, featuring the picture of a naked, prepubescent girl with slashes of light coming from her crotch. My children could get, if they wished, from newsstands, mail order, or video stores, a staggering assortment of pornography.

I was out of college and in a park in Athens when I first saw a man exhibiting himself in public. In our local grocery store a man dropped his pants in front of Emily and Katy when I was just a few aisles away.

When I was in high school we exchanged shocked whispers about a friend's sister who had gotten in trouble and had to get married. By the time Emily was a senior she knew that several of her friends were having sex regularly with their boyfriends and that they considered it no big deal.

Twenty years ago a friend cried on my shoulder because her husband had stepped out on her. I have spent hours lately talking to a woman whose husband buys sex magazines and visits all the women whose phone numbers are listed, crossing the names off one by one. He hides the magazines, but she always finds them, and then he promises it's over, but it never is.

When I was growing up someone had brazenly carved a bad word on a large rock in the hills above our home and I stared at it in stunned fascination. Any day that I choose to visit my children's schools and walk down the halls or across the playground, my ears are pelted with the "F" word until they're bruised.

When I was about twelve I took down the dictionary when I knew no one else was in the house and cautiously looked up the word "pubic." About that same age Emily bounced in from school, saying, "Mom, what's 'oral sex?' Is that when you just talk about it?"

When I was young the newspapers sometimes carried stories of rape and once or twice a year something terribly bizarre. On our front pages today are stories of ritual sexual abuse of children by Satan worshipers who are, on the surface, perfectly respectable citizens, and a local lawyer who accidentally drowned a prostitute in his bathtub in a game of bondage, and the making of "snuff" pornographic movies in which the actresses are, we're told, actually killed before the cameras.

What do you do? Has the world gone nuts? How, *how* do you

help your children make their way in sexual sanity through the maze of a crazy world?

And how do you keep them from getting the idea that it's normal, that it's okay, that that's just the way the world is? Few things are shocking anymore. We have become numb, barely blinking at dreadful things, and shrugging our shoulders at things that are unspeakable. Oh, I want my children to be shocked, to be outraged that that's what the world has come to. I want them not to stand for it.

What do you do?

I don't want just to turn back the clock. I don't want for my children a world in which the joy of sexual experience must be laden with guilt. I don't want for anybody the world in which the Victorian bride was discovered by her husband on their wedding night, lying across the bed, a handkerchief drenched in chloroform held to her nose and a note pinned to her nightgown: "Mama says to go ahead and do to me as you want."

I don't want for Katy and Emily a world in which their sexual needs are not taken as seriously as the sexual needs of men, and where their opportunities in life are so limited that they have to trade sexual duty for sustenance, even to a respectable husband. That world was no good.

I don't even want for my children the world I grew up in, in the forties and fifties. In spite of living on a farm I had no idea that human beings did anything like what I saw cows and bulls doing. I had to read about human sexual activity from the marriage manuals on the shelves of the places I babysat when I was a teenager, and I was absolutely amazed. Even as an adult I still didn't know enough about human sexuality to prevent my thinking that the cure for homosexuality was marriage.

I don't want my children to be that innocent. And they're not.

"Come quick!" yells Katy beside the cage of the hamsters she's breeding. "Quick, you guys! They're doing it! They're doing it!"

I don't mind. It is pretty interesting. And I make sure they know from age three that human bodies are designed for a similar kind of joining, but that for us it involves much more than it does for animals.

We are setting the table for supper one evening when Aaron asks Katy why she had stayed home from school that day.

"I was sick," she says. "I had a headache and I threw up."

"Hmmmmm," says John wisely, having just passed the health-class test that I had quizzed him on. "Sounds like gonorrhea to me."

"John! Please!"

"Ha!" laughs Aaron. "Katy doesn't even know what gonorrhea is!"

"I do too," says Katy, offended.

"What is it?"

"It's when your pooh is runny!"

Teaching moments. I grab them all, this one to make sure Katy knows what gonorrhea is and how you prevent it; another one to make sure the boys know that the child of a homosexual man is no more likely to be gay than anybody else; another one to discuss what it means when the sunny, enthusiastic daughter of a friend of mine has sex with her boyfriend *one* time and gets pregnant and has to drop out of school, her life changed forever; or when a sixteen-year-old we know runs away from home for three months and comes back pregnant and old; or when a divorced man we know has an affair with a woman who gets pregnant and he is stuck for the next eighteen years paying child support to a woman he doesn't love, for a child he never wants to see.

Or when we learn that still another friend of the family has been diagnosed with AIDS. We add him to our family prayers, but we know the sorrow that is coming.

Or when Mother Teresa speaks to the graduating class at Harvard, encouraging them to premarital chastity. Or when Ann

Landers prints yet another good letter about the results of "decisions made below the navel."

I sprinkle stories and discussions across my children's minds like seeds and hope they will take root.

Not just the scary stories—the good stories too. I tell them about my brother Don who, after a three-month marriage that did not take, spent years alone. It was not until his mid-forties that he was lucky enough to find Susie, who already had three children, and who told me this story. Don had always yearned to be a father. He was good with the three he had inherited, but he wanted also to create a child of his own.

After a period of adjustment they issued the invitation and a few weeks later, when Susie thought it was probably accomplished, they hurried out to the drugstore and bought a kit to test for pregnancy. After they prepared the solution and went through all the necessary steps, Susie rested on the bed while Don took it into the bathroom to observe the results.

He didn't come out for a very long time. Susie waited and waited. Finally she called out to him, "Don? What does it say?"

A few minutes later Don appeared in the doorway, tears running down his cheeks. "It says . . . it says that I'm going to be a daddy!" Then he walked over to the bed, knelt down, put his hands on Susie's abdomen, and gave his little baby a blessing. Then he put his hands on Susie's head and gave her a blessing.

What if every baby was invited into the world like that? I hope my children remember that story. They watch their Uncle Don playing with Kimberly, who is the light of his life, and I know the image is stronger than the image on the cover of *Virgin Killers*.

Certainly my children live in a world that is more dangerous, more truly crazy, than the world I grew up in. But they're far better prepared than I was to meet their world.

So far so good. The kids seem to be knowledgeable and content and following the family rules. And the mother? She follows them too. Most divorced women, I know, do not sleep alone all the time. I see articles in the magazines about how to let your children know or not know that you're having men overnight and how to get the most out of your sexual adventures as a single person. I have also read plenty of articles on the disenchantment of the uncommitted sexual encounter, on emotional burnout, and on more and more singles opting for celibacy. There have been plenty of overnight guests in this house: couples, families, single women, single men. But it has never occurred to the children, I believe, to wonder about the sleeping arrangements of their mother.

I have yearnings I do not discuss with them. I have had temptations I do not discuss with them. But I draw the line, because if I don't then how can I expect my children to? And I think there's some general universal law that says life works best this way.

I do what I can and pray a lot and am grateful for good fortune and know we're not out of the woods yet. You can control your own home, your own teachings, your own example, but all of a sudden you realize *the world* is out there, waiting to do battle.

Like the Dial-a-Porn messages that until recently anybody could get if they called a certain number on the telephone. When I saw an unrecognized "service" number on my monthly billing and called it to hear Tina begin to deliver her fantasy of the day, I slammed down the phone and assembled the children.

"All right, who called the sex-talk number?" I demanded.

John and Aaron snickered and looked at each other. "I didn't," said Aaron.

"John?"

"Tim made me dial it. He didn't tell me what it was. He told me it was real funny and dared me to do it."

"And *was* it real funny?" I asked indignantly.

"It was *hilarious*! I couldn't believe how funny it was!"

"Well, John, you'll have to find your laughs somewhere else. That call cost me fifty cents. If the number appears ever again, it will cost you ten dollars. And who dialed it the second time? Who did it?" All four looked at me innocently and shook their heads. "Nobody? It must have been the little elf who leaves apple cores on the piano. Is that how he gets his kicks? Okay, my dears. *The end.*"

I got off easy. Recently I read in the local newspaper that a man was suing the phone company because his son, in one month, racked up an eight-hundred-dollar phone bill to such a number.

———

The yearbook incident, when Aaron was just finishing seventh grade, struck even closer to home. That year a number of girls had been calling him on the phone. One girl in particular, Judy, seemed to be calling him daily. It was annoying, and often I made him cut the calls short, but it was not a major problem. He didn't spend time with Judy or the other girls except at school, and I didn't think there was anything to worry about. They were probably nice girls.

It was Emily, I think, who called my attention to it. "Mom," she said soberly, sitting down on the couch in my bedroom. "I think you'd better look at Aaron's yearbook."

"Why?"

"Just because."

I walked to Aaron's room and opened the door. "Aaron?" He wasn't there. A stack of books and papers was on the floor and I knelt down beside it, reaching under the science book and the red binder and the English workbook to pick up the white yearbook with red lettering: W.C.I., '84.

I had a whole stack of yearbooks from my junior high and high school, very much like the one I now held in my hand. The last several days of school were spent going from friend to friend to have them write some fun little statement and sign their names. "You're a real sweet kid and it was fun to have chorus with you. Don't sing too much over the summer and strain your vocal cords. Ha, ha!"

I had looked through a yearbook of my mother's and found the sentiments of the early 1900's, "When skies are grey and you are blue, just think of me, a friend that's true."

I opened Aaron's seventh grade yearbook. "Hi, Aaron. You're a real sweetie. But whatever you do, don't get Judy pregnant this summer. I know a f— is a f—, but that's going too far."

I could not believe what I was reading. Did I dare to turn the page? "Hi, Aaron, you totally cool guy. Don't get laid too much this summer. You might get a little sore. Luv ya."

And across from that a full page signed by Judy, a lengthy obscene appreciation of Aaron's body and an exaggerated description of what she wished they could do over the summer.

I was heartsick as I closed the book. Seventh grade. Aaron was twelve! Those girls were twelve! How did they get so brazen? How dare they write such things in a yearbook? I wanted to slap Judy, slap her girlfriends, lecture their parents, tell them all to keep their garbage to themselves.

When I saw Aaron an hour later I had calmed down a bit.

"So what did you look in the book for anyway?" he asked defensively. "It's *my* book!"

"That's true, and you belong to this family and this is my business too. Why did those girls write such things?"

"It's a joke, Mom. A stupid joke. They think it's funny."

"Did you write anything like that in Judy's?"

"Of course not. It's stupid."

"Aaron . . . how do you . . . behave with those girls at school?"

Aaron laughed in embarrassment. "You mean, do I lead them on or something? No. They're just kind of crazy."

"Well, Aaron, I am really uncomfortable with you having those things in your yearbook. A yearbook is something you want to share with other people to show them your year at school. Something you want to be able to show your children. Would you like your children to read what those girls wrote?"

Aaron thought for a moment. "No."

"What can you do about it?"

"Where's the white-out, Mom?"

Emily has lived the longest and learned the most on this subject, I think, of any of the children. Case history of Emily: She is not only beautiful—tall and blond and charming and witty and talented—but she needs very much to love and to be loved. She takes this very seriously.

There were a few minor crushes in grade school, but the first major one occurred when she was eleven and fell for Bennett, whom she had met while all the kids performed in *A Christmas Carol*. After yearning for a couple of weeks to see him again, she got John to call him on the phone to see if he might want to go to the movies on Saturday afternoon with all of them. She rehearsed John carefully on what he was to say. He was *not* to say that Emily put him up to it, and he was to be *very* cool and casual. They went upstairs to my telephone to call. In a few minutes Emily came flying down the stairs.

"Do you know what Johnny did?" she screamed in horror. "He said, 'Bennett, Emily wants to know if you want to go to the movies with us.' And then Aaron called out, 'She's scared to ask you herself. *She loves you!* '" Emily threw herself onto the couch. "Now I'll never see him again," she sobbed. "I'll neve see him again."

The boys came down the stairs giggling.

"Don't even speak to me," shouted Emily as she ran out of the room. "I hate you! I hate you! You do not exist!"

The boys did not exist for hours. In fact, that evening I overheard Emily speaking to Katy in the other room in sad, sad tones. "Katy, we do not have any brothers."

Before the day was done the boys had apologized and Emily had reluctantly reinstated them in the family. She never went to the movies with Bennett, and a few weeks later she was talking about somebody else. That was her first heartbreak—simple, dramatic, and easily healed.

––––––––

A couple of years and several crushes later, when Emily noticed that some of the other girls at school had breasts and she did not, the plot began to thicken. Something, at least, was thickening, but it did not do Emily any good. She watched and waited and felt and measured and compared and rejoiced when the right swelling caught up with the left swelling, and mourned when all swelling stopped, and was outraged.

I tried to keep things light. "Sorry, Em. You got it from me. Or, rather, you *didn't* get it from me. Did I tell you about the time last month when I went in for a mammogram and the doctor told me they couldn't find anything, and I said, 'Which, a tumor or a breast?' "

Emily smiled against her will. "Very funny, Mom."

"Let me tell you, Em, there are plenty of successful flat-chested women. Ballet dancers *can't* have big breasts. And I had this friend in college who had less than *you* do, and she got a great husband. Mollie had so little she had to have special bras made in Salt Lake City. She found that they made great pin cushions, and this one day while she was sewing, the doorbell rang. Well, it was her boyfriend, who was *stunned* to see two dozen pins stuck in her left breast. Kinky, huh?"

Emily's salvation, during her days of slow development, was

her ability to joke about it. Once when we were eating a chicken dinner, Katy asked, "Is the chicken all white meat?"

"No," I replied, "the breast is white and the rest of the chicken is dark."

Emily hung her head in despair. "Oh, no," she said. "I'm all dark meat!"

———

I guess she was about fifteen when I started getting worried. Her hormones were functioning normally, as were her interests, and Emily began asking me, "What's *wrong* with having sex before you get married, Mom? I mean, I know what you've always said, but what's really *wrong* with it? I mean if two people love each other. . . ."

Once she came bouncing into my bedroom. "Mom? Gina wants to know if I can spend the night at her house. She's going to have some boys over and she said anybody who wants to can go to bed with them."

My eyebrows shot up, but my voice remained low. "Oh, really? Well, do you *want* to go?"

Emily burst into laughter. "Are you kidding? That is too gross! Makes me throw up!"

I sighed in relief, but the next week Emily turned pensive again. "I honestly don't see what's wrong with it. I mean, if you're really in love, I hear it can strengthen your relationship."

"Oh? Where do you hear that?"

"A friend at school."

"Who?"

"You don't know her."

"She's in love?"

"Oh, Mom, she is *so* much in love. I am so jealous."

"And they're having sex?"

"Yes. And she says it's wonderful. It's made them feel so close."

"Really?"

"I am so jealous."

———

About then I started hating slumber parties. Why had I ever allowed Emily to sleep anywhere but in her own bed? She should be locked up after dark until she's twenty-one. What did all those teenage girls boiling with hormones talk about until three or four in the morning? And did some of them have boys over too? Horror stories of teenage sex orgies went through my mind. I envisioned Emily coming to me sobbing, telling me she was pregnant, telling me she had syphilis, telling me she'd had an abortion. She was just at a slumber party losing too much sleep and eating too many potato chips, for heaven's sake, but my mind wouldn't stop. Emily was remarkably open with me, but what things was she not telling me? Certainly she wouldn't do anything stupid. She was a smart girl. But she was only fifteen!

One night I heard her speaking in a low voice on the telephone. "I'm sorry. Gee, I'm sorry. . . . It'll be okay. . . . You'll get over it. Oh, I'm sorry."

After she hung up, she sat staring at the phone for a minute. I went over and sat down beside her. "What's the matter, Em?"

"Nothing," she began, then changed her mind. "This . . . friend of mine . . . had an abortion."

"Oh."

"Her boyfriend was real religious. It just about killed him. They broke up."

"Oh, Em."

Emily stared at her hands in confusion. "She loved him *so much*."

"I know," I lied.

———

I don't want my children's friends to make mistakes just so my children can learn from them. Why can't everyone learn from listening? But it never has been and it never will be, and at least I'm grateful that Emily's learning from others' mistakes.

She learned a lot in the next couple of years. And I began to sleep better when she was at a slumber party. Once she came into my room at two in the morning and sat down on my bed.

"Mom?"

"Where you been, Em?"

"With Joanne. She is such a mess, and it makes me so mad! Her boyfriend is such a jerk, Mom, a real jerk. She doesn't even enjoy it, but she thinks she *has* to have sex with him or he won't be her boyfriend anymore. So she does and she hates it. She is so dependent on him. Why is she so *dependent* on him?"

"Centuries of programming."

"Well, I told her she has to shape up and think more of herself. She's got to figure out who *she* is *now*, or what kind of a wife will she be? Or mother? I told her she has to learn what love is, real love, not just sex. I told her sex clouds your thinking. I'm certainly not going to give that much of myself to some guy who doesn't respect me. Oh, Mom, men can be such jerks. And women can be so dumb!"

———

Many people may find it strange that a parent should hope for and even expect premarital chastity from her children—though perhaps it does not sound so strange today as it did a few years ago. Today the Federal Office of Adolescent Pregnancy is calling for teenage abstinence to combat the huge problem of abortion and of children giving birth to children. And the Surgeon General is asking for the same thing to help fight the AIDS epidemic. "The message," they say, "is do not engage in sex until marriage." Considering the horror of AIDS alone, it may be that premarital chastity will become one of the most prized qualities in the marriage market.

———

The first writing project I did after my book *Good-bye, I Love You*, was *A Time to Love*, a musical program that celebrates premarital chastity. When I gathered the children one night in Emily's bedroom and read it through and played a tape of the music, Emily exploded with excitement.

"That is *so neat*, Mom," she said. "Can I direct that for the church? Can I?"

Emily threw on her shoes and went running out the door and up to the bishop's house to get permission. Two months later seven hundred people watched Emily and a dozen other beautiful young people sing and speak of the joys of romantic love and the pitfalls of premature sex. "To everything there is a season, and a time to every purpose under heaven: a time to be born, and a time to die; a time to plant and a time to pluck up that which is planted; a time to weep and a time to laugh; a time to embrace and a time to refrain from embracing; a time to love."

By coincidence, that was the weekend a CBS camera crew was at our home to interview me for the Charles Kuralt Sunday Morning News, and they were able to get some footage of the program. At the end of the evening, during the tremendous applause, I heard one of the cameramen turn to the producer and sigh, "Boy! Wouldn't it be nice if life could really be like this?"

You're never out of the woods quite. But the woods get scarier and scarier, and you have to try.

14. "We're Not All Brothers!"

As I opened my mouth to tell the joke, I suddenly decided to change the person in it from a man to a woman. There was no reason it should be a woman, but there was no reason it should be a man in the first place.

I had heard the joke begin like this: "A man goes into the hospital and he sees three patients. . . ." But in my sudden burst of affirmative action, I told it like this. "A woman goes into the hospital and she sees three patients . . ." It was a token gesture, but it gave me a little satisfaction.

Later that week when some guests were over for dinner, Emily brightly turned to me. "Can I tell that joke, Mom? The one about the hospital?"

"Sure."

"Okay," Emily grinned, putting down her chicken leg. "This man goes into the hospital and he see three patients . . ."

I stared at her, speechless. Emily, how *could* you? *You* heard the joke told about a *woman*, and without even noticing you changed it to a joke about a *man*! I felt stabbed in the back, furious, and terribly sad, not at what Emily had done to the joke but at what the *world* had done to *Emily*! Here she was only eight and already she had been carefully programmed to hold up the male standard, to see, to speak in male terms.

We're constantly reassured that "man" (including "woman," of course) means "mankind." But when school children are told to draw pictures of "man" as human being, "man" as differentiated from animals or trees, they consistently—both girls and boys—draw pictures of males. And here Emily had done the same thing. Male-centered thinking, centuries old, had entered my door without knocking and made itself right at home.

———

But things are changing. Today old concepts are being challenged, and, in spite of the dangers, I for one am thrilled. I don't want to dump my four children into a sexless pot and stir and pour them out all alike. I love Virginia Woolf's wise statement, "Men and women *are* different. What needs to be made equal is the value placed on those differences." We're not there yet. But we're working on it.

I watch my own children, and other people's children, toss around terribly important questions like balls on the playground. Just how this new game is shaping up, what the rules will be, how much of a say all players will get, if there will have to be winners and losers—all this is yet to be seen. But I love to watch, and here are some of the best stories I've gathered about how children are experiencing maleness and femaleness in today's word. Good stories and bad stories—which are which depends on your own point of view.

In first grade, Emily came in and said, "Glen and I were playing that we were getting ready for our wedding, only he started taking charge and told me I couldn't be an actress, I had to just stay home and be a housewife, so I broke our engagement!"

When my friend Pat's ten-year-old boy got a paper route, the first thing he bought was a Cabbage Patch Doll. Right away he brought it to his mother and said, "Will you make some combat fatigues for my doll out of camouflage, so I can put them on it in case I get any flak?" He now has a lot of different outfits for his doll, some very macho and some quite feminine.

Which reminds me of the time we were at the church Christmas party and John, age three, sat on Santa's lap and asked for a doll. A man standing next in line chuckled and said to me, "You better watch out, next year he'll be wanting a dress." The man then smiled as he watched his own boy ask Santa Claus for a tank and a gun.

At supper one evening I handed Aaron a news clipping. "Your turn, Aaron. Read."

" 'Since the Chinese government's decree that couples may have just one child, authorities are alarmed at the increase in infanti . . .' "

"Infanticide."

"What's that?"

"Keep reading."

"In one rural area near the central China city of Wuhan a survey revealed that, among the under fives, there were 503 boys to every 100 girls. In some places the ratio is even higher, 8 to 1. There can be only one explanation: parents are,' " Aaron's eyes blinked wide and his voice rose, " '. . . killing their baby daughters?' "

"Ohhh," whimpered Katy.

"That's dumb," said John.

"*Mom!*" Emily slammed her fork across the table and stood up. "Will you quit making us read these *depressing* articles?"

"I can't, Emily."

"Well, they make me *so* mad!"

An obstetrician I know said once, "It really makes me boil, what I see happening sometimes. A woman will take an amniocentesis test and find out the sex of the baby, and if it's not what she wants she'll ask for an abortion. I don't do it and neither do most doctors I know but more women want to abort a girl baby than a boy."

A woman I know is a state supreme court judge. Her little girl said, in amazement, when she was told that Mr. So and So was also a judge, "But I thought all judges were mommies!"

Overheard at a PTA dinner: "Yes, Cindy wants to be a pilot, just like her dad."

My neighbor asked me the other day, "Why does my son make a big deal about washing the dishes? He says it's woman's work. But he sees his father washing dishes all the time! Where does he get that?"

Katy brought in the mail and looked at an envelope and laughed. "Mrs. Gerald Pearson! *Mrs.* Gerald Pearson! Gerald's not a Mrs."

"No, Katy," I said, "that's for me."

"For you? Your name isn't Gerald."

"Married women are often called by their husband's name."

"They are? Why?"

"Well, to show . . . that they belong together. Actually, to show that she belongs to him."

"That's dumb. I don't know why women have to change their names anyway."

"Mostly just to keep things organized so families can have the same name."

"Well, then they should just flip a coin to see which name they're going to use."

———

A friend had to take her five-year-old daughter to the restroom at the airport. But as the mother opened the door that had a picture of a skirted female on it, the little girl said, "Mom, we can't go in here. We're wearing pants!"

———

Not long ago John went out on his very first real date. *She* invited *him* to dinner and a concert, and she drove in her car, picking him up and bringing him home. The tickets had been a gift to her, and she suggested that they go dutch for dinner.

———

"Mom," eight-year-old Emily whispered at me with a frown as we sang in church, "Onward, Christian Soldiers." "Look. 'Brothers all are we.' *We're not all brothers!*"

———

A hundred students were asked to visualize as vividly as possible ninety-three animals and then to note whether each was male or female. Ninety-eight percent of the students said buffaloes are male. The most female animal, at ninety-four percent, was the butterfly.

———

John: Hey, Mom, here's a joke you'll like.

Me: Let me have it.

John: This guy goes into a drugstore and looks around and finally picks out a box of Tampax. The druggist says, "Are you sure that's what you want?" The guy says, "You bet! Says right here on the box that with these you can swim, ride, or play tennis, and up to now I haven't been able to do *any* of those things!"

———

Once, when I was spending some time with a man twelve years younger than me, John said, "Mom, you can't go out with Tom. He's far too young for you."

Aaron replied, "So what? Uncle Don is lots older than Aunt Susie."

———

Emily at ten came up to ask me a question and stood behind me for a moment while I typed. She read over my shoulder. " 'Eve was created out of Adam's rib.' Adam's rib? You're kidding!"

"That's what it says in the Bible. You know about Adam and Eve."

"Yeah, but not about the *rib*. Or else I forgot. I thought they were created at the same time out of the same stuff!"

"Well, the Bible says Eve was made from Adam's rib."

"Hmpf!" Emily turned on her heel and left. "I like my way better."

———

At a school in Arizona not long ago a teacher punished an eleven-year-old boy by making him parade around school in a dress.

———

Melissa: Sure I want to be a mommy when I grow up, but then I also want to do something *really important*!

———

I was proud of Aaron for being the first one to come up with the answer to the riddle. If you've heard this riddle, skip it, but if you haven't heard it, you need to. You'd be amazed how many extraordinarily bright minds can't get it.

"A man and his son (in this riddle it *does* have to be a man) are out driving and they get into a terrible automobile crash. The father is killed. The boy is rushed to the emergency room of the hospital and taken up to surgery. The surgeon walks in and looks at the patient and says, 'I can't operate on this boy. This boy is my *son!*' Who is the surgeon?"

"What?" says John. "Say that again."

"The surgeon?" puzzles Katy.

"Impossible!" says Emily.

"Easy," grins Aaron. "The surgeon . . . is the *mother!*"

A friend who works in a young women's sports program complained to me, "The budget for the boys' programs is always twice what it is for the girls', and the boys always get to do the funnest stuff. Whenever I complain about that or about anything really, the men smile and say, 'Remember who's in charge here.' And there always has to be a man supervising, as if women don't have a brain in their heads."

Emily: Mom, do you know what Rhonda's fiancé said to her? He said that after they're married she'll have to submit to him and do what he wants because that's what it says in the Bible.

Me: And what do you think of that?

Emily: I think that any man who would say something like that ought to be shot!

One evening when Emily was about eleven, the boys were nine and eight, and Katy was four, I opened up the book I had checked out from the library, *Children's Letters to God*, and read to them. "Dear God, are boys really better than girls? I know you *are* one, but try to be fair."

Emily giggled and John smiled a little.

"How do you suppose God would answer that letter?" I asked.

John responded quickly. "I think God would say something like 'Even though I happen to be a boy, of course boys and girls are equally better.' "

"Yeah, something like that," agreed Emily.

Aaron shrugged his shoulders. Katy was too little to care.

"Well," I said, "I think the reply to this letter might be, 'You are mistaken. To assume that God is a boy is to tell only half the story. God is Father and Mother, just as your own parents are. God is as much girl as boy, as much woman as man. Heavenly Father *and* Heavenly Mother.' "

"What?" interrupted Aaron vehemently. "*Mother?* Heavenly *Mother?* There's no such thing. There's Heavenly *Father*, but that's *all!*"

I was not prepared for his strong reaction. "How do you know that, Aaron?" I asked.

"*Everybody* knows that!"

"Everybody used to know the earth is flat."

"Well, I've seen pictures. They showed us pictures in Sunday school, and God is a *man!*"

"Well, who *drew* those pictures?" asked Emily, always ready to take Aaron on. "*Men* drew those pictures."

John jumped in. "Of course God's a man. Didn't you see *The Ten Commandments?*"

When Katy was nine, I opened up the birthday present she had wrapped for me. "You are really going to like this, Mom," she said excitedly.

I held up a small plastic sign: WHEN GOD CREATED MAN—SHE WAS ONLY JOKING.

Last year Emily came home from her "Women in Motion Pictures" class and said, "Those films are getting so depressing. All the women in the stories hate men. And all the women in the class seem to hate men, and even the teacher does. I'm sick of it. I don't hate men! And I don't want to fight anybody about anything. Let's just get on with life!"

15. The Pine Wood Derby

I knew it was coming, and I hated the thought: The Cub Scout Pine Wood Derby. It came annually, not like Christmas or Easter or the bursting of the magnolia tree in the front yard. It came like the April fifteenth tax deadline or the mess the olive tree makes on the back deck or my Pap smear.

The Pine Wood Derby: an evening of racing miniature cars, carved from small blocks of wood. I did not pay much attention that first year when the boys brought home their car kits from their pack meeting. It looked simple enough. Carve to the shape you want. Attach the little plastic wheels. Paint a design on it. Glue a penny or two underneath to make it close to the weight maximum. Okay. Clearly I could not be much help with the cars, but the boys could figure it out for themselves. I promptly forgot the whole thing.

And the boys did too until three days before the event.

"Mom, do we have a drill?" Aaron spoke from behind me as I filled up the dishwasher.

"Not that I know of," I said absently. "Why?"

"My car. I need to drill a hole underneath for the weights."

"Hmmm. Guess you'll just have to use your pocket knife."

"Do we have any sinkers?"

"Sinkers? Like for fishing? Why?"

"To glue inside the hole for weights."

"What's wrong with pennies?"

"I need pennies *and* sinkers. Bob says if the weight isn't *exactly* right the car won't go as fast."

"Really? It has to be exact, huh?"

"Bob says."

"Well, I think there's some fishing stuff in the bottom drawer out in the garage."

"And then will you drive me and John down to the store to weigh our cars?"

I stopped loading the dishwasher and looked at Aaron's serious face. He held out for my observation the roughly carved, unpainted body of a little car. "Weigh them?" I asked. "On the produce scales?"

"Yeah."

"They have to be that exact? Just for a little Cub Scout race?"

"Bob says."

———

The evening of the derby the boys grabbed their cars and jumped into the old Volvo station wagon. John had had his under a fan for a couple of hours to make sure the paint was dry. His car, the "Ripper," was black with a white stripe running down the middle, and Aaron's, the "Speed Demon," was green with yellow dots all over it. John's had accidentally been split in half, but glue and paint had solved the problem. The cars and the boys all looked happy, if a little slipshod. Tomorrow I'd have to take John for another haircut. Didn't we go just last week?

"Hi, Carol Lynn." Diana, the den mother, was at the recreation hall, greeting. I liked Diana a lot, a very capable, generous, cheerful woman. "Welcome to the derby."

I looked over her shoulder and felt my mouth fall open. Filling the hall was a huge, sloping track with four lanes. Lighted numbers flashed above each lane. One. Two. Three. Four.

Diana laughed. "Is this your first derby?"

"Yes."

"Quite a setup, isn't it?"

"Looks like something out of Las Vegas."

Diana laughed again and led me over to the track. "The old system was pretty primitive. Two men had to judge the cars as they crossed the finish line, and that led to plenty of arguments, you can believe me. So one of our electrical engineers came up with this system. See? When a car goes under the light here at the bottom it triggers an impulse to the sign up above the tracks, and we know instantly who came in first, second, third, and fourth."

Aaron and John stared at the sophisticated setup and then down at their humble little cars. "Wow!"

"It makes for a pretty interesting evening. And tonight I think things are going to be *very* interesting."

"Oh?"

"There's a saying around the Cub Scout offices. If the *boys* walk in carrying the cars it'll be a good derby. If the *fathers* walk in carrying the cars there's going to be trouble." She sighed and rolled her eyes. "Take a look."

I glanced around. Several boys were holding their cars, as my sons were. But eight or nine men stood, each with a little car in his open palm, shooting curious glances at each other's creations and doing last minute inspections on his own.

Why hadn't John and Aaron enlisted their father's help when

he was with us the Saturday before? He had probably been a Cub Scout once. Maybe he could have given them a few pointers or made the cars look a little more professional. But they'd gone to a movie on Saturday and nobody had even thought about the cars. As I looked around at the boys with their fathers, I felt the stab of envy I had often felt since Gerald and I had separated. And maybe even a little bitterness. How would it be for a boy to have his father around on Monday? On Wednesday? How would it be for a boy to be able to say, "When Dad gets home tonight."

"Hey, Diana," boomed a big voice to our right. "Where do we weigh in at?"

I turned to see Brother Hansen holding carefully in his outstretched hand a car that made us all gasp. It looked like something lifted from a showroom floor and shrunk, perfect in every detail. No Mercedes ever had a more gorgeous silver luster. Brother Hansen's round face shone as brightly as his car. His little boy Tony trailed after him.

"Pretty good, huh?" he boomed again. "Meet the winning car, ladies. 'The Atomic Blast.' I spent four hours at the library researching the most aerodynamically sound shape, and this is it. Hey, Paul!" Brother Hansen intercepted another man carrying a car. He was trailed by his ten-year-old boy. "I told you I'd be back this year and beat the socks off you, you old son of a gun!" Both men laughed.

"Nice car," said Brother Mitchell, a tall man who always looked more at home in the recreation hall than he did in the chapel.

"You better believe it. You just better believe it!"

Brother Mitchell reached out to pick up the Atomic Blast, but Brother Hansen pulled the car back violently. "No!" he shouted, then recovered with a laugh. "*Mine!* No touching. These wheels are balanced just the way I want them. Any little bump can throw things off. That's what happened to my car last year and it's not going to happen again!"

"Well, you got yourself a race, Brother. This little car ain't no slouch either." He held up his sleek, red race car. "We call her the 'Killer.' Isn't that right, Ben?" With his free hand he punched the shoulder of his son.

"You bet! 'The Killer'!"

The two men, trailed by the two boys, marched over to the weigh-in table.

———

As we took our places to watch the event, I felt transported. I was not at a Cub Scout social; I was at an ancient tribal ritual. Fathers and sons were gathered here to pit their manly thrust against others' manly thrusts and *win*! The men were at war as they always are, and the women cheered them on as we always do.

Most of it was done in good spirit. Even the losers cheered the winners. Usually, and at the beginning. But as the stakes rose so did the tension. Each car had at least four chances to prove itself, one in each lane. Cheers or moans greeted each car's performance as it shot into first or second place, pushed into third or pooped into fourth, or (humiliation of all humiliations) stopped halfway down the track, just stopped dead. As various cars were eliminated the boys good-naturedly took their little autos and sat down to watch the rest of the race. Aaron's was the fifth car eliminated and John's the seventh. Both of them took it well. But, as Diana had predicted, when a car was eliminated that had been carried in by a *father*, losing was a different story.

"There's something wrong on track four! My car did great on the other three tracks! It was the *track*!"

"Wait! I don't think they started them all right. Mine didn't start with the others. Didn't you see that?"

"Come on, you lousy little block of wood. Cream 'em! Knock 'em off the track! Kill 'em!"

Brother Hansen's Atomic Blast did very well for itself, and so did the Killer. Both cars were still in the running as the race approached its final quarter, and both men stood closer and closer to the track, their faces and their fists getting tighter and tighter.

What was it Alan Alda had said about male competition? "Society is suffering from testosterone poisoning." Yes. I could feel it in the room. The testosterone level was getting higher and higher. We needed to open some windows.

The bell rang and four cars went zooming down the track. Then only three were zooming. One was slowing, just slowing as if a tiny driver inside had put on the brakes. The Atomic Blast was stopping.

"No!" screamed Brother Hansen. "No!" He closed his eyes and grabbed his hair. Whoops or groans came from the onlookers. When Brother Hansen opened his eyes, the Atomic Blast had stopped three quarters of the way down, and lane four was blinking a bright "1" signaling the triumph of the Killer.

Brother Mitchell jumped up and down and laughed. "Whooooeeee! The Atomic Blast really *bombed*, didn't it? Yup!"

Instantly Brother Hansen pushed his way to the starting place. "Somebody must have bumped my car," he shouted, the veins bulging in his temples and neck like I had seen them do once before when he had caught a group of young deacons letting the air out of his tires in the parking lot. "Somebody must have put it down too hard at the starting line and wrecked the balance. I demand we run that one again!"

Boos erupted from several of the men. "Come on, Hansen," called out Brother Mitchell. "You lost. Take it like a man!"

"Run it again!" insisted Brother Hansen.

"Sorry," said one of the two men in charge, dismissing him with a gesture and preparing the next set of cars.

Fuming and muttering, Brother Hansen pushed his way back to the spot on the track where the Atomic Blast had stopped and with great embarrassment removed it as one would remove a puppy that had defecated on the neighbor's front porch. Then he stomped toward the exit. His son grabbed his arm.

"No, Dad. Don't go."

Brother Hansen's free hand gripped his son's wrist and propelled him along toward the door.

"But I don't want to go, Dad. I want to watch. It's fun! I want to watch!"

Brother Hansen paused at the exit, then leaned up against the doorway to watch from a distance. And frown.

I walked over to Diana, whose hands were clasped tightly to her chest. "Are you praying?" I asked.

She laughed. "You see what I mean? Actually, I do pray during the races. I pray that the boy who most needs to win will win."

"Does it happen?"

"Often. Last year a kid who had felt like a real loser won, and it changed his whole self-image."

"Who needs to win today?"

"I'm not sure. But I'm not praying for the Killer. Any car but the Killer."

"Next year let's make our boys name their cars something like . . . oh, 'Kindness,' 'Mercy,' 'Charity.' "

Diana threw back her head and laughed. "Let's do it!"

A giant shout brought our attention back to the track. The race was over, and Diana stood on tiptoe to see who had won. "Oh, yay!" she smiled, "Bill won. I'm so glad." She rushed off to prepare the awards.

And, from the doorway, Brother Hansen frowned.

Later that night as the boys and I sat on the bar stools dunking graham crackers in milk, I asked John, "So what do you think? Do you want to race again next year?"

"Sure," he said brightly. "It was fun!"

"You, Aaron?"

"Yeah. Only . . ."

"Only what?"

"Only next year I'm going to win. It's putting graphite on the wheels that does it. Next year I'll put graphite on the wheels."

Aaron's little green car with the yellow dots sat on the counter beside his graham crackers. I had helped write out the ribbons so that each boy would go home having won something. "Most Original." "Most Colorful." "Most Mysterious." By the time we had come up with twenty adjectives we were hysterical. John's had received "Most Interesting," and Aaron's was dubbed, "Brightest." But "Brightest" doesn't warm you through the night. "Winner" does.

"Hey, Diana, I want to talk to you," I said over the phone the next morning. "Do you want to go for a walk?"

"Sure. When?"

"Now."

The "black road" for joggers and walkers and strollers (all of which I have been, in that order) seems to go on endlessly in Walnut Creek. There are beautiful places to walk, but when I walk and talk every tree and flower goes by unnoticed.

"Listen. I was really blown away by the event last night. Why do we do this to our boys? It's crazy, it's so competitive, so . . . unbrotherly. For somebody to be a *winner* means that everybody else has to be *losers*. And these are just kids! Isn't there a better way?"

Diana sighed. "I've thought that too. But I finally decided it was just as well to initiate them into the real world. That's what they're going to have to meet out there. But we should try to cushion it, so that they learn everybody wins some and loses some—and teach them to do both gracefully."

"Like Brother Hansen?" I added. "Why don't they keep the fathers out of it? Why isn't there a rule that says fathers cannot even *touch* the cars?"

"The idea is to give boys the experience of working with a man to learn how to use tools and such."

"But, Diana, some boys *do not have a man* who lives with them. What about them? What about John and Aaron and the other boys who don't have a father around and who might have a mother who can't even tell a hammer from a screwdriver, such as your present company?"

"That's why we have car clinics."

"Car clinics?"

"I guess you didn't hear about them. Several of the fathers invite any boy who wants to to bring his car over and get help with it. It doesn't really make a whole lot of difference. You saw how Brother Hansen's car bombed out after the ninety million hours he put into it. If you get the wheels on right, the rest is pure luck. But working with one of the other fathers is a nice thing for the boys and makes them feel a little more confident. I'm sorry you didn't hear about it. Next year send them over to Ted Sutton's. He's great."

"But is the whole thing really worth it?"

"The boys would scream to high heaven if we dropped the derby. But I will admit . . ." she smiled and shook her head. "I will admit that when this last baby turned out to be a boy, one of the first things I said to myself was 'Oh, no. *Three more Pine Wood Derbies!*' "

About February was when I started dreading it. Any week now the boys would bring home those miserable little kits and start talking about winning, which, because of their inadequate mother, they never could.

The day came, of course, not too long in fact after the annual olive mess on the back deck. The boys rushed in with their car kits and dropped them in front of me on the kitchen counter.

"This time," said Aaron, "this time I'm going to do it right! Where can we get some graphite, Mom?"

I felt that familiar rush. I didn't know where to get graphite. I didn't even know what graphite was. I wouldn't know graphite if it stood up and bit me. "I'm not sure, Aaron," I said, "but we'll find out."

Who had Diana told me to call for that . . . what did they call it? Car clinic. Ted Sutton. Yes. He was a sweet, approachable man, with warm eyes and curly brown hair. And I judged that his testosterone level was about right. I could call him.

"Brother Sutton?" I said, when I got him on the phone that evening. "This is Sister Pearson."

"Hi. How ya doin'?"

"Okay. Listen. I'm one of those single mothers you may have read about."

"Yeah?"

"And I've got two boys and two car kits and a lot of personal frustration, and I was told that you . . ."

"You bet! Saturday afternoon, one to five, bring 'em over!"

As I walked up the driveway to Ted's garage to pick up the boys that Saturday, I paused for a moment to watch six or seven youngsters busily involved in car clinic, sawing, sanding, painting, drilling.

"Hey, Mom, look!" John held up his car. "All done but the painting. Neat, huh?"

"Great!"

Aaron held up his, spinning one of the wheels with a finger. "I sanded the wheels good before I put on the graphite. That's one of the secrets Brother Sutton told us. Sometimes there's little spurs on the wheels. You got to sand them. *Then* put on the graphite."

"Aha!"

As the boys gathered up their things, I watched Ted help Larry Bennion, another boy without a father at home. Larry's dark brown hair fell over his eyes as he carefully attached the wheels to his car. His plaid shirtsleeves were rolled up, a small nail was in place between his teeth, and Ted's large, sure hands were guiding the boy's smaller ones through the process of building. This was ritual, too, handing down tribal wisdom. There was, in this open garage, no "Mine!"

Down the table a ways, waiting in line for his father's attention, was Ted's son Bryce. That's how it was for me in fourth grade, too, when my mother was my school teacher out in Gusher. She had to call on everybody else before she called on me or it would look like she was playing favorites. "Well, Bryce," I said. "What a good man you are to share your father like this."

He smiled and shrugged. "We had fun."

Fun. I'm sure they did, I thought to myself, and it probably never even occurred to him once that for every other kid his father helped, his own chances of winning went down a notch. Now all the other boys knew the secret of sanding the wheels for possible spurs before you put on the graphite.

The Pine Wood Derby that year was not so colorful as the year before. If we'd had to come up with a ribbon to describe it, it would not have been "Most Exciting." Possibly "Most Wonderful."

Brother Hansen and Brother Mitchell had graduated from the Cub Scout program. And Diana had instituted a sportsmanship award, to be given equal honor with the racing award. The fathers seemed to be in the background where good fathers belonged. And the boys, bright-eyed and holding their little pine wood treasures as if they were the crown jewels, eagerly put their cars in the lineup and took their places to watch. Twenty or so boys—blond, dark, thin, chubby, T-shirted, sweatshirted, scout-shirted, lanky, short—crowded close around the race track to fuel their little cars with psychic energy and cheers and maybe a prayer or two. I watched the boys and I watched the crowd and I watched Brother Sutton. He clapped for his own son and he clapped for everybody else's sons with a marvelous equality.

Except at the very end. I think he clapped for Larry Bennion, who finished in first place, even harder than he clapped for Aaron Pearson, who finished second, and even harder than he clapped for Bryce Sutton, who finished third. I think he even whistled and stomped when Larry, grinning and amazed, shuffled up and shook his head and reached out his hand to receive the award.

Next day I wrote a letter.

Dear Bryce,

Last night as I watched you receive third prize in the derby, it occurred to me that you might easily have received first prize if your dad had not helped the other boys and had helped only you.

And I wanted to write to make sure you know that any boy who has a dad like yours won first prize a long time ago.

16. The End of the World

The end of the world was supposed to happen on Monday, April 29, 1980. I first received the information from ten-year-old John, who burst into the kitchen, out of breath and wide-eyed.

"Says who?" I demanded, continuing to cut up carrots for the chicken soup.

"All the kids at school."

"Yeah? What do they know?"

"It's true, Mom," John said passionately. "Even my teacher heard somebody taking about it on the radio."

"Hold it. Where does this come from? End of the *world*?"

"This guy in Montana who's a psychic says that on April twenty-ninth there will be a nuclear attack that will be the beginning of the end. Remember Pearl Harbor? This guy predicted it to the very day! He said a whole year ahead of time that the Japanese were going to bomb Pearl Harbor and exactly when it would be. Then he disappeared, but now he's back and he lives in Montana and he says that April twenty-ninth will start the end of the world!"

John shifted his weight back and forth as if he had to go to the bathroom, but I knew it was much more serious. I walked over close to him and looked into his eyes. They were pools into which unwelcome stones had been thrown, troubling the waters. Did John really believe this? Did my son actually think that he, that all of us, had only a couple of weeks left to live?

"John," I said, "I don't believe that. This is nothing new. One group or another has *always* been busy ushering in the end of the world. I know of a group that sold all their possessions and went up on a mountain to await the end of the world on a certain day. And you know what happened?"

"What?" John's troubled eyes were riveted on mine.

I leaned in close. "Nothing. Absolutely nothing. Except the sun came up and the sun went down just like it's doing today. Finally they realized they'd been duped and came down off the mountain and went about their business."

John considered this a moment, then spoke again. "But it's going to happen sometime, Mom. Now that we've got the bomb, it's *got* to happen. This guy was right about Pearl Harbor. And Khomeini's crazy. They've still got our hostages and he must be pretty mad that we tried that airlift."

"John, I'm not sure what's going to happen on April twenty-ninth. But I know what's going to happen on April thirtieth."

"What?"

"I'm going to take you out to dinner. Anywhere you want to go. And we're going to celebrate the world going on and on."

John was silent. "Mom," he finally said, "couldn't we go on April twenty-eighth?"

That night I paused at the door of the children's bathroom. "Visiting hours are over," I said, as I usually did. And, as usual, the children paid no attention. What should have been a seven-minute ritual of brushing teeth and washing faces often expanded into a full-blown party. There was John on the floor and Aaron and Katy on the counters, laughing through their toothpaste as Emily performed yet another of her impressions of their most colorful school teacher.

"Class, class," she intoned, posing pompously and flaring her nostrils. "Who can tell me . . . ? Son," she interrupted herself, pointing at Aaron, "Son, what are you laughing at?" A white spray of Pepsodent spewed from Aaron's mouth as he broke into a huge laugh.

"Thanks, Aaron," said Emily as Emily, wiping her face and arm with a towel, then dashing a glass of water at Aaron.

Squeals. Screams. Giggles. Yells. Life, life as it should be. Life as it was for me and now for my children, and as it will be for their children, surely as it will be for their children.

John had temporarily forgotten the end of the world. A ten-year-old can so easily be seduced by the charms of life. But I knew the dark thoughts were still there, the fears, and that they would evidence again, maybe in a bad dream tonight, maybe in a sad stare tomorrow.

Emily had been thinking about the end of the world too, about the millennium, that thousand years of peace and joy in which heaven and earth finally become friends. It wasn't the millennium that troubled her but the terrible times we'd have to go through to get there. Once she and I had sat out in the parking lot during Sunday school because she didn't want to go in. The lesson the week before had been on the millennium.

"I don't want it to come," said Emily, looking at me fiercely.

"I don't want just the people who are righteous to be lifted up and the rest to be burned to a crisp."

"Oh, Emily," I said, "whatever is coming, I think that God will work things out in a just and kind way. I can't get too worried about the Judgment."

"But it says in the Scriptures that the world will be burned. It says that terrible things will happen. And I don't like it one bit."

Aaron never said much about his fears. He was too macho for that, even at age eight. Once, however, he had appeared in my bedroom in the middle of the night, dragging his sleeping bag and settling down at the foot of my bed.

"What's the matter, Aaron?" I asked.

"I'm freaked," he answered.

"About what?"

"About the past."

He never made clear just what about the past freaked him, but a kid who can get freaked about the past can probably get freaked about the future, so I figured even Aaron was not above fearing the end of the world.

Had Katy even thought about such things? She was only five. The other night when she and I were getting ready to say her prayers, I said to her, "You know, Katy. I don't believe that God is up there in the sky somewhere. I think God is just here, around us."

"Around us," Katy said thoughtfully. "Just like ring-around-the-rosies. And when God falls down, that's the end of the world."

The end of the world! Even a five-year-old could say the words, could hold the thought.

Is that what was going to happen? Was God going to fall down? Were *we* going to fall down, fall down so badly that we would bring everything crashing down with us and all that would be left would be dark ash sifting through empty places where children should have been laughing and having water fights and giving impressions of their most colorful teachers?

That could happen. I could still remember the moment unspeakable horror became reality in my mind. I was about fifteen and I was watching the movie *Judgment at Nuremberg*. Suddenly there came on the screen actual film clips of the atrocities of World War II, piles of dead bodies, real human beings slaughtered by Hitler. Spencer Tracy was acting. Burt Lancaster was acting. Judy Garland was acting. But those others, those men and women and children whose thin and twisted bodies lay in stark, shocking piles, they were *not* acting. I had to close my eyes. And that was the day my innocence was gone forever.

It *could* happen. This was our legacy to our children, a world in which it *could* happen. I remember something John had said to me when he was about five. We were visiting the rather disorderly home of a young couple we knew. John took a look around and asked, "Do you have any children?" "No," the woman responded. "Then who made this mess?" John demanded.

We have made a very big mess, and it is our children who are going to have to deal with it.

The end of the world might not happen, probably would not happen, on April 29, but there were some fears here that I felt had to be addressed. I called the children into my bedroom and said, "Look, we need to talk about this end-of-the-world business. Not only does it not have to happen on April 29, it doesn't *have* to happen *anytime*. Do you remember Jonah?"

"Yeah," said Emily. "He got swallowed by the whale."

"But something else. The story goes that God told Jonah to prophesy to the people of Ninevah that they would be destroyed in forty days because they were so wicked and violent."

"You mean, God would *kill them all* just for being bad?" asked Aaron incredulously.

"No. God knew they would kill themselves by being bad, so he told Jonah to go tell them they were going to die. Well, do you know what they did?"

"What?"

"They believed him. And they repented. They quit being so wicked and violent. And they were not destroyed. Actually that made Jonah mad because he prophesied something and it did not happen. But I think it's wonderful, because it proves, you guys, that nothing *has* to happen. We can change the destiny of the world if we shape up and quit being so violent. Maybe somehow the millennium can come in like a sunrise."

"Well, we've only got two weeks," said John.

"Ninevah only had forty days," I replied.

"But what can we do about it," asked John in exasperation. "We're just little kids."

Emily dropped to her knees. "I know," she sighed. "Pray and mediate. Again!"

Ever since the hostages had been taken, we had remembered them in our family prayers and I had led the children in visualizations of the hostages returning to their families, of President Carter and Khomeini shaking hands, of people all over the world shaking hands and singing and dancing together.

"Anything else?" I asked as we got up.

"Emily can quit being so violent and quit punching me and stuff," volunteered Aaron.

"Well, we can all repent," I said. "Anytime we feel like punching or shoving or anything like that, we can remember that we need to be part of the solution and not part of the problem."

"Like my being nice to Aaron is going to save the world!" snorted Emily.

"It's a start," I said.

———

I did not count down the days, but John did, and the evening of April 28 found him quite emotional. The kids on the playground had continued to talk about the prediction, and so had some people on the radio. It was mostly treated as a joke, but some were taking it seriously. Like John.

"It's the Iranian thing that's going to do it, Mom," he said. "Khomeini might kill us all, even if he has to go too."

"I think it's lame about the prophecy," said Aaron as we all headed upstairs. "How does a guy in Montana know anything about the end of the world? He doesn't even live in New York or anything."

I climbed into bed and looked at the stars and the moon out my window. Stars were eternal, certainly. The moon was, wasn't it? And the world that we rode, surely, surely that would last forever, wouldn't it, somehow? I wouldn't be here forever, I knew that. But I would rise in some other sky, some other life. So why couldn't I just close my eyes and go to sleep? If the world was really careening toward its end, it surely wouldn't happen tomorrow.

I was furious with myself for even thinking about it. It was stupid, of course. I sometimes read the new year prediction in the *National Enquirer*, and they *never* happened. Oh, once in a while something did. And, well, Jeane Dixon *had* tried very hard to get a message to John F. Kennedy that November not to go to Dallas. Khomeini didn't have the bomb, did he? What if . . . ? What would I do if I knew this were really our last day?

I pulled back the covers, climbed out of bed, and walked into the hall. The children were asleep, each in their own bedroom. Katy's room was first. I went in. Juliet, her cat, was curled inside the circle of her arm. A five-year-old face is pure enough by daylight, but by moonlight it is sweet to break your heart. What if . . . ?

I knelt down and put my hands on Katy's head. That's what I

would do if I knew this would be our last day together. I would give her a blessing.

"Dear Father and Mother in Heaven," I said softly. "I don't think the world is going to end tomorrow. But just in case, and if it ever does, thank you for Katy and for all her beauty and for letting us be together. And please bless her and keep her always. Katy, I love you very much and I bless you with peace and comfort and strength to meet whatever life gives you. . . ."

When I was through, I went to John's room and knelt by his bed and did the same. Then to Emily's room, and Aaron's. Then I went back to bed and I slept.

On April 30, as John and I sat at a table at the Sizzler and waited for our order of steak and shrimp, John said to me thoughtfully, "Mom, I didn't ever tell you about the killer bees, did I?"

"The what?"

"When I was five and we were still in Utah, some kid I knew told me that there was a swarm of killer bees that was coming up from Mexico and it would take them three years to get here and when they did it would be all over for everybody."

"And you believed him?"

"I sure did. I thought that eight was as old as I was ever going to get. For three years I thought that."

"Really, John? Why didn't you tell me this?"

"I didn't want you to worry."

"Well, John," I laughed and held up my water glass, "to today. And to lots of tomorrows. May they go on forever."

John raised his glass and smiled. "Or at least until I'm as far over the hill as you are."

When I found a package containing copies of a painting an artist friend, Ingo Swann, had done, and saw the title, "Millennium,"

I called out, "Emily! Run quick, Em. The millennium has come! Hurry!"

In a moment she poked her head in my door and asked suspiciously, "What did you say?"

"Look." I handed her the picture. It was ocean and sky. Huge waves jubilantly rose up to frame a rising sun. Shooting stars celebrated. It was warm. It was a picture of birth, not of death.

A smile crept over Emily's face and her eyes shone. "This is beautiful!" she said. "It's peaceful! The millennium could really come like this, feel like this?"

"Why not? Maybe, if we all just wake up, we can skip over the cataclysm."

"Can I keep this, Mom?"

"Sure."

Emily has Ingo's "Millennium" picture on her wall along with her James Dean and Marilyn Monroe pictures. And I have mine above my computer along with a large poster of my favorite Greek island.

Maybe the people of Jonah's day really did save Ninevah. Maybe we can save the world. Maybe Emily and John and Aaron and Katy will have children who will have children.

ABOUT THE AUTHOR

CAROL LYNN PEARSON's book *Good-bye, I Love You* was published in 1986. Her four books of poetry have sold more than a quarter of a million copies and her poems have been widely reprinted. In 1984 she won first prize in the Bay Area Poet's Competition. Born in Salt Lake City, with a strong Mormon pioneer heritage, Ms. Pearson draws on that background for much of her writing. In addition to poetry, plays and other books, Ms. Pearson has written educational motion pictures and magazine articles, is a popular public speaker, and serves on an advisory board to the National AIDS Task Force on the treatment of AIDS patients. She lives in northern California with her family.